ARMENIA	AUSTRALIA	AUSTRIA	AZERBAIJAN	BAHAMAS	BAHRAIN	BANGLADESH
A-HERZEGOVINA	BOTSWANA	BRAZIL	BRUNEI	BULGARIA	BURKINA FASO	BURMA
CHILE	CHINA	COLOMBIA	COMOROS	CONGO	CONGO (DEM. REP.)	COSTA RICA
ICAN REPUBLIC	ECUADOR	EGYPT	EL SALVADOR	EQUATORIAL GUINEA	ERITREA	ESTONIA
GEORGIA	GERMANY	GHANA	GREECE	GREENLAND	GRENADA	GUATEMALA
ICELAND	INDIA	INDONESIA	IRAN	IRAQ	IRELAND	ISRAEL
KIRIBATI	KOREA, NORTH	KOREA, SOUTH	KUWAIT	KYRGYZSTAN	LAOS	LATVIA
MACAU	MACEDONIA	MADAGASCAR	MALAWI	MALAYSIA	MALDIVES	MALI
MONGOLIA	MOROCCO	MOZAMBIQUE	NAMIBIA	NAURU	NEPAL	NETHERLANDS
PAKISTAN	PANAMA	PAPUA NEW GUINEA	PARAGUAY	PERU	PHILIPPINES	POLAND
OMÉ & PRÍNCIPE	SAUDI ARABIA	SENEGAL	SEYCHELLES	SIERRA LEONE	SINGAPORE	SLOVAK REPUBLIC
ST LUCIA	ST VINCENT	SUDAN	SURINAM	SWAZILAND	SWEDEN	SWITZERLAND
DAD & TOBAGO	TUNISIA	TURKEY	TURKMENISTAN	TUVALU	UGANDA	UKRAINE
VENEZUELA	VIETNAM	WESTERN SAMOA	YEMEN	YUGOSLAVIA	ZAMBIA	ZIMBABWE

PHILIP'S

FAMILY
WORLD ATLAS

PHILIP'S

FAMILY
WORLD ATLAS

IN ASSOCIATION WITH
THE ROYAL GEOGRAPHICAL SOCIETY
WITH THE INSTITUTE OF BRITISH GEOGRAPHERS

Published in Great Britain in 2000
by George Philip Limited,
a division of Octopus Publishing Group Limited,
2–4 Heron Quays, London E14 4JP

Cartography by Philip's

ISBN 0–540–07786–0

A CIP catalogue record for this book is available from the British Library.

Printed in China

Details of other Philip's titles and services can be found on our website at: www.philips-maps.co.uk

Philip's is proud to announce that its World Atlases
are now published in association with The Royal
Geographical Society (with The Institute of British
Geographers).

The Society was founded in 1830 and given a
Royal Charter in 1859 for 'the advancement of
geographical science'. It holds historical collections
of national and international importance, many of
which relate to the Society's association with and
support for scientific exploration and research
from the 19th century onwards. It was pivotal
in establishing geography as a teaching and research
discipline in British universities close to the turn of
the century, and has played a key role in geographical
and environmental education ever since.

Today the Society is a leading world centre for
geographical learning – supporting education, teaching,
research and expeditions, and promoting public
understanding of the subject.

The Society welcomes those interested in geography
as members. For further information, please visit the
website at: www.rgs.org

Contents

World Statistics: Countries

This alphabetical list includes all the countries and territories of the world. If a territory is not independent, then the country it is associated with is named. The area figures give the total area of land, inland water and ice.

The units for areas and populations are thousands. The population figures are 1998 estimates. The annual income is the Gross National Product per capita in US dollars. The figures are the latest available, usually 1997.

COUNTRY/TERRITORY	AREA km² 1,000s	AREA miles² 1,000s	POPULATION 1,000s	CAPITAL	ANNUAL INCOME US $
Afghanistan	652	252	24,792	Kabul	600
Albania	28.8	11.1	3,331	Tirana	750
Algeria	2,382	920	30,481	Algiers	1,490
American Samoa (US)	0.20	0.08	62	Pago Pago	2,600
Andorra	0.45	0.17	75	Andorra La Vella	16,200
Angola	1,247	481	11,200	Luanda	340
Anguilla (UK)	0.1	0.04	11	The Valley	6,800
Antigua & Barbuda	0.44	0.17	64	St John's	7,330
Argentina	2,767	1,068	36,265	Buenos Aires	8,750
Armenia	29.8	11.5	3,422	Yerevan	530
Aruba (Netherlands)	0.19	0.07	69	Oranjestad	15,890
Australia	7,687	2,968	18,613	Canberra	20,540
Australian Ant. Terr. (Aus.)	6,120	2,363	0	–	–
Austria	83.9	32.4	8,134	Vienna	27,980
Azerbaijan	86.6	33.4	7,856	Baku	510
Azores (Portugal)	2.2	0.87	238	Ponta Delgada	–
Bahamas	13.9	5.4	280	Nassau	11,940
Bahrain	0.68	0.26	616	Manama	7,840
Bangladesh	144	56	125,000	Dhaka	270
Barbados	0.43	0.17	259	Bridgetown	6,560
Belarus	207.6	80.1	10,409	Minsk	2,150
Belgium	30.5	11.8	10,175	Brussels	26,420
Belize	23	8.9	230	Belmopan	2,700
Benin	113	43	6,101	Porto-Novo	380
Bermuda (UK)	0.05	0.02	62	Hamilton	31,870
Bhutan	47	18.1	1,908	Thimphu	390
Bolivia	1,099	424	7,826	La Paz/Sucre	950
Bosnia-Herzegovina	51	20	3,366	Sarajevo	300
Botswana	582	225	1,448	Gaborone	4,381
Brazil	8,512	3,286	170,000	Brasilia	4,720
Brunei	5.8	2.2	315	Bandar Seri Begawan	15,800
Bulgaria	111	43	8,240	Sofia	1,140
Burkina Faso	274	106	11,266	Ouagadougou	240
Burma (= Myanmar)	677	261	47,305	Rangoon	1,790
Burundi	27.8	10.7	5,531	Bujumbura	180
Cambodia	181	70	11,340	Phnom Penh	300
Cameroon	475	184	15,029	Yaoundé	650
Canada	9,976	3,852	30,675	Ottawa	19,290
Canary Is. (Spain)	7.3	2.8	1,494	Las Palmas/Santa Cruz	–
Cape Verde Is.	4	1.6	399	Praia	1,010
Cayman Is. (UK)	0.26	0.10	35	George Town	20,000
Central African Republic	623	241	3,376	Bangui	320
Chad	1,284	496	7,360	Ndjaména	240
Chatham Is. (NZ)	0.96	0.37	0.05	Waitangi	–
Chile	757	292	14,788	Santiago	5,020
China	9,597	3,705	1,236,915	Beijing	860
Christmas Is. (Australia)	0.14	0.05	2	The Settlement	–
Cocos (Keeling) Is. (Aus.)	0.01	0.005	1	West Island	–
Colombia	1,139	440	38,581	Bogotá	2,280
Comoros	2.2	0.86	545	Moroni	450
Congo	342	132	2,658	Brazzaville	660
Congo (Dem. Rep. of the)	2,345	905	49,001	Kinshasa	110
Cook Is. (NZ)	0.24	0.09	20	Avarua	900
Costa Rica	51.1	19.7	3,605	San José	2,640
Croatia	56.5	21.8	4,672	Zagreb	4,610
Cuba	111	43	11,051	Havana	1,300
Cyprus	9.3	3.6	749	Nicosia	13,420
Czech Republic	78.9	30.4	10,286	Prague	5,200
Denmark	43.1	16.6	5,334	Copenhagen	32,500
Djibouti	23.2	9	650	Djibouti	850
Dominica	0.75	0.29	78	Roseau	3,090
Dominican Republic	48.7	18.8	7,999	Santo Domingo	1,670

COUNTRY/TERRITORY	AREA km² 1,000s	AREA miles² 1,000s	POPULATION 1,000s	CAPITAL	ANNUAL INCOME US $
Ecuador	284	109	12,337	Quito	1,590
Egypt	1,001	387	66,050	Cairo	1,180
El Salvador	21	8.1	5,752	San Salvador	1,810
Equatorial Guinea	28.1	10.8	454	Malabo	530
Eritrea	94	36	3,842	Asmara	570
Estonia	44.7	17.3	1,421	Tallinn	3,330
Ethiopia	1,128	436	58,390	Addis Ababa	110
Falkland Is. (UK)	12.2	4.7	2	Stanley	–
Faroe Is. (Denmark)	1.4	0.54	41	Tórshavn	23,660
Fiji	18.3	7.1	802	Suva	2,470
Finland	338	131	5,149	Helsinki	24,080
France	552	213	58,805	Paris	26,050
French Guiana (France)	90	34.7	162	Cayenne	10,580
French Polynesia (France)	4	1.5	237	Papeete	7,500
Gabon	268	103	1,208	Libreville	4,230
Gambia, The	11.3	4.4	1,292	Banjul	320
Georgia	69.7	26.9	5,109	Tbilisi	840
Germany	357	138	82,079	Berlin/Bonn	28,260
Ghana	239	92	18,497	Accra	370
Gibraltar (UK)	0.007	0.003	29	Gibraltar Town	5,000
Greece	132	51	10,662	Athens	12,010
Greenland (Denmark)	2,176	840	59	Nuuk (Godthåb)	15,500
Grenada	0.34	0.13	96	St George's	2,880
Guadeloupe (France)	1.7	0.66	416	Basse-Terre	9,200
Guam (US)	0.55	0.21	149	Agana	6,000
Guatemala	109	42	12,008	Guatemala City	1,500
Guinea	246	95	7,477	Conakry	570
Guinea-Bissau	36.1	13.9	1,206	Bissau	240
Guyana	215	83	820	Georgetown	690
Haiti	27.8	10.7	6,781	Port-au-Prince	330
Honduras	112	43	5,862	Tegucigalpa	700
Hong Kong (China)	1.1	0.40	6,707	–	22,990
Hungary	93	35.9	10,208	Budapest	4,430
Iceland	103	40	271	Reykjavik	26,580
India	3,288	1,269	984,000	New Delhi	390
Indonesia	1,905	735	212,942	Jakarta	1,110
Iran	1,648	636	64,411	Tehran	4,700
Iraq	438	169	21,722	Baghdad	2,000
Ireland	70.3	27.1	3,619	Dublin	18,280
Israel	27	10.3	5,644	Jerusalem	15,810
Italy	301	116	56,783	Rome	20,120
Ivory Coast (Côte d'Ivoire)	322	125	15,446	Yamoussoukro	690
Jamaica	11	4.2	2,635	Kingston	1,560
Jan Mayen Is. (Norway)	0.38	0.15	1	–	–
Japan	378	146	125,932	Tokyo	37,850
Johnston Is. (US)	0.002	0.0009	1	–	–
Jordan	89.2	34.4	4,435	Amman	1,570
Kazakstan	2,717	1,049	16,847	Astana	1,340
Kenya	580	224	28,337	Nairobi	330
Kerguelen Is. (France)	7.2	2.8	0.7	–	–
Kermadec Is. (NZ)	0.03	0.01	0.1	–	–
Kiribati	0.72	0.28	85	Tarawa	920
Korea, North	121	47	21,234	Pyŏngyang	1,000
Korea, South	99	38.2	46,417	Seoul	10,550
Kuwait	17.8	6.9	1,913	Kuwait City	17,390
Kyrgyzstan	198.5	76.6	4,522	Bishkek	440

COUNTRY/TERRITORY	AREA km² 1,000s	AREA miles² 1,000s	POPULATION 1,000s	CAPITAL	ANNUAL INCOME US $
Laos	237	91	5,261	Vientiane	400
Latvia	65	25	2,385	Riga	2,430
Lebanon	10.4	4	3,506	Beirut	3,350
Lesotho	30.4	11.7	2,090	Maseru	670
Liberia	111	43	2,772	Monrovia	770
Libya	1,760	679	4,875	Tripoli	6,510
Liechtenstein	0.16	0.06	32	Vaduz	33,000
Lithuania	65.2	25.2	3,600	Vilnius	2,230
Luxembourg	2.6	1	425	Luxembourg	45,360
Macau (China)	0.02	0.006	429	Macau	7,500
Macedonia	25.7	9.9	2,009	Skopje	1,090
Madagascar	587	227	14,463	Antananarivo	250
Madeira (Portugal)	0.81	0.31	253	Funchal	–
Malawi	118	46	9,840	Lilongwe	220
Malaysia	330	127	20,993	Kuala Lumpur	4,680
Maldives	0.30	0.12	290	Malé	1,080
Mali	1,240	479	10,109	Bamako	260
Malta	0.32	0.12	379	Valletta	12,000
Marshall Is.	0.18	0.07	63	Dalap-Uliga-Darrit	1,890
Martinique (France)	1.1	0.42	407	Fort-de-France	10,000
Mauritania	1,030	412	2,511	Nouakchott	450
Mauritius	2.0	0.72	1,168	Port Louis	3,800
Mayotte (France)	0.37	0.14	141	Mamoundzou	1,430
Mexico	1,958	756	98,553	Mexico City	3,680
Micronesia, Fed. States of	0.70	0.27	127	Palikir	2,070
Midway Is. (US)	0.005	0.002	2	–	–
Moldova	33.7	13	4,458	Chişinău	540
Monaco	0.002	0.0001	32	Monaco	25,000
Mongolia	1,567	605	2,579	Ulan Bator	390
Montserrat (UK)	0.10	0.04	12	Plymouth	4,500
Morocco	447	172	29,114	Rabat	1,250
Mozambique	802	309	18,641	Maputo	90
Namibia	825	318	1,622	Windhoek	2,220
Nauru	0.02	0.008	12	Yaren District	10,000
Nepal	141	54	23,698	Katmandu	210
Netherlands	41.5	16	15,731	Amsterdam/The Hague	25,820
Neths Antilles (Neths)	0.99	0.38	210	Willemstad	10,400
New Caledonia (France)	18.6	7.2	192	Nouméa	8,000
New Zealand	269	104	3,625	Wellington	16,480
Nicaragua	130	50	4,583	Managua	410
Niger	1,267	489	9,672	Niamey	200
Nigeria	924	357	110,532	Abuja	260
Niue (NZ)	0.26	0.10	2	Alofi	–
Norfolk Is. (Australia)	0.03	0.01	2	Kingston	–
Northern Mariana Is. (US)	0.48	0.18	50	Saipan	11,500
Norway	324	125	4,420	Oslo	36,090
Oman	212	82	2,364	Muscat	4,950
Pakistan	796	307	135,135	Islamabad	490
Palau	0.46	0.18	18	Koror	5,000
Panama	77.1	29.8	2,736	Panama City	3,080
Papua New Guinea	463	179	4,600	Port Moresby	940
Paraguay	407	157	5,291	Asunción	2,010
Peru	1,285	496	26,111	Lima	2,460
Philippines	300	116	77,736	Manila	1,220
Pitcairn Is. (UK)	0.03	0.01	0.05	Adamstown	–
Poland	313	121	38,607	Warsaw	3,590
Portugal	92.4	35.7	9,928	Lisbon	10,450
Puerto Rico (US)	9	3.5	3,860	San Juan	7,800
Qatar	11	4.2	697	Doha	11,600
Réunion (France)	2.5	0.97	705	Saint-Denis	4,500
Romania	238	92	22,396	Bucharest	1,420
Russia	17,075	6,592	146,861	Moscow	2,740
Rwanda	26.3	10.2	7,956	Kigali	210

COUNTRY/TERRITORY	AREA km² 1,000s	AREA miles² 1,000s	POPULATION 1,000s	CAPITAL	ANNUAL INCOME US $
St Helena (UK)	0.12	0.05	7	Jamestown	–
St Kitts & Nevis	0.36	0.14	42	Basseterre	5,870
St Lucia	0.62	0.24	150	Castries	3,500
St Pierre & Miquelon (Fr.)	0.24	0.09	7	Saint Pierre	–
St Vincent & Grenadines	0.39	0.15	120	Kingstown	2,370
San Marino	0.06	0.02	25	San Marino	20,000
São Tomé & Príncipe	0.96	0.37	150	São Tomé	330
Saudi Arabia	2,150	830	20,786	Riyadh	6,790
Senegal	197	76	9,723	Dakar	550
Seychelles	0.46	0.18	79	Victoria	6,850
Sierra Leone	71.7	27.7	5,080	Freetown	200
Singapore	0.62	0.24	3,490	Singapore	32,940
Slovak Republic	49	18.9	5,393	Bratislava	3,700
Slovenia	20.3	7.8	1,972	Ljubljana	9,680
Solomon Is.	28.9	11.2	441	Honiara	900
Somalia	638	246	6,842	Mogadishu	500
South Africa	1,220	471	42,835	C. Town/Pretoria/Bloem.	3,400
Spain	505	195	39,134	Madrid	14,510
Sri Lanka	65.6	25.3	18,934	Colombo	800
Sudan	2,506	967	33,551	Khartoum	800
Surinam	163	63	427	Paramaribo	1,000
Svalbard (Norway)	62.9	24.3	4	Longyearbyen	–
Swaziland	17.4	6.7	966	Mbabane	1,210
Sweden	450	174	8,887	Stockholm	26,220
Switzerland	41.3	15.9	7,260	Bern	44,220
Syria	185	71	16,673	Damascus	1,150
Taiwan	36	13.9	21,908	Taipei	12,400
Tajikistan	143.1	55.2	6,020	Dushanbe	330
Tanzania	945	365	30,609	Dodoma	210
Thailand	513	198	60,037	Bangkok	2,800
Togo	56.8	21.9	4,906	Lomé	330
Tokelau (NZ)	0.01	0.005	2	Nukunonu	–
Tonga	0.75	0.29	107	Nuku'alofa	1,790
Trinidad & Tobago	5.1	2	1,117	Port of Spain	4,230
Tristan da Cunha (UK)	0.11	0.04	0.33	Edinburgh	–
Tunisia	164	63	9,380	Tunis	2,090
Turkey	779	301	64,568	Ankara	3,130
Turkmenistan	488.1	188.5	4,298	Ashkhabad	630
Turks & Caicos Is. (UK)	0.43	0.17	16	Cockburn Town	5,000
Tuvalu	0.03	0.01	10	Fongafale	600
Uganda	236	91	22,167	Kampala	320
Ukraine	603.7	233.1	50,125	Kiev	1,040
United Arab Emirates	83.6	32.3	2,303	Abu Dhabi	17,360
United Kingdom	243.3	94	58,970	London	20,710
United States of America	9,373	3,619	270,290	Washington, DC	28,740
Uruguay	177	68	3,285	Montevideo	6,020
Uzbekistan	447.4	172.7	23,784	Tashkent	1,010
Vanuatu	12.2	4.7	185	Port-Vila	1,290
Vatican City	0.0004	0.0002	1	–	–
Venezuela	912	352	22,803	Caracas	3,450
Vietnam	332	127	76,236	Hanoi	320
Virgin Is. (UK)	0.15	0.06	13	Road Town	–
Virgin Is. (US)	0.34	0.13	118	Charlotte Amalie	12,000
Wake Is.	0.008	0.003	0.3	–	–
Wallis & Futuna Is. (France)	0.20	0.08	15	Mata-Utu	–
Western Sahara	266	103	280	El Aaiún	300
Western Samoa	2.8	1.1	224	Apia	1,170
Yemen	528	204	16,388	Sana	270
Yugoslavia	102.3	39.5	10,500	Belgrade	2,000
Zambia	753	291	9,461	Lusaka	380
Zimbabwe	391	151	11,044	Harare	750

World Statistics: Cities

This list shows the principal cities with more than 500,000 inhabitants (only cities with more than 1 million inhabitants are included for Brazil, China and India). The figures are taken from the most recent census or estimate, and are the population of the metropolitan area, e.g. greater New York, Mexico or Paris. All the figures are in thousands. Local name forms have been used for the smaller cities (e.g. Kraków).

AFGHANISTAN
Kabul 1,565
ALGERIA
Algiers 2,168
Oran 916
ANGOLA
Luanda 2,418
ARGENTINA
Buenos Aires 11,256
Córdoba 1,208
Rosario 1,118
Mendoza 773
La Plata 642
San Miguel de
Tucumán 622
Mar del Plata 512
ARMENIA
Yerevan 1,248
AUSTRALIA
Sydney 3,770
Melbourne 3,217
Brisbane 1,489
Perth 1,262
Adelaide 1,080
AUSTRIA
Vienna 1,595
AZERBAIJAN
Baku 1,720
BANGLADESH
Dhaka 6,105
Chittagong 2,041
Khulna 877
Rajshahi 517
BELARUS
Minsk 1,700
Homyel 512
BELGIUM
Brussels 948
BENIN
Cotonou 537
BOLIVIA
La Paz 1,126
Santa Cruz 767
BOSNIA-HERZEGOVINA
Sarajevo 526
BRAZIL
São Paulo 16,417
Rio de Janeiro 9,888
Salvador 2,211
Belo Horizonte 2,091
Fortaleza 1,965
Brasília 1,821
Curitiba 1,476
Recife 1,346
Pôrto Alegre 1,288
Manaus 1,157
Belém 1,144
Goiânia 1,004
BULGARIA
Sofia 1,116
BURKINA FASO
Ouagadougou 690
BURMA (MYANMAR)
Rangoon 2,513
Mandalay 533
CAMBODIA
Phnom Penh 920
CAMEROON
Douala 1,200
Yaoundé 800
CANADA
Toronto 4,344
Montréal 3,337
Vancouver 1,831
Ottawa-Hull 1,022
Edmonton 885
Calgary 831
Québec 693
Winnipeg 677
Hamilton 643
CENTRAL AFRICAN REP.
Bangui 553
CHAD
Ndjaména 530
CHILE
Santiago 5,067
CHINA
Shanghai 15,082
Beijing 12,362
Tianjin 10,687
Hong Kong (SAR)* 6,502
Chongqing 3,870
Shenyang 3,860
Wuhan 3,520
Guangzhou 3,114
Harbin 2,505
Nanjing 2,211
Xi'an 2,115
Chengdu 1,933
Dalian 1,855
Changchun 1,810
Jinan 1,660
Taiyuan 1,642
Qingdao 1,584
Fuzhou, Fujian 1,380
Zibo 1,346
Zhengzhou 1,324
Lanzhou 1,296
Anshan 1,252
Fushun 1,246
Kunming 1,242
Changsha 1,198
Hangzhou 1,185
Nanchang 1,169
Shijiazhuang 1,159
Guiyang 1,131
Ürümqi 1,130
Jilin 1,118
Tangshan 1,110
Qiqihar 1,104
Baotou 1,033
Hefei 1,000
COLOMBIA
Bogotá 6,004
Cali 1,985
Medellin 1,970
Barranquilla 1,157
Cartagena 812
CONGO
Brazzaville 937
Pointe-Noire 576
CONGO (DEM. REP. OF THE)
Kinshasa 1,655
Lubumbashi 851
Mbuji-Mayi 806
COSTA RICA
San José 1,220
CROATIA
Zagreb 931
CUBA
Havana 2,241
CZECH REPUBLIC
Prague 1,209
DENMARK
Copenhagen 1,362
DOMINICAN REP.
Santo Domingo 2,135
Santiago 691
ECUADOR
Guayaquil 1,973
Quito 1,487
EGYPT
Cairo 9,900
Alexandria 3,431
El Gîza 2,144
Shubra el Kheima 834
EL SALVADOR
San Salvador 1,522
ETHIOPIA
Addis Ababa 2,112
FINLAND
Helsinki 532
FRANCE
Paris 9,319
Lyon 1,262
Marseille 1,087
Lille 959
Bordeaux 696
Toulouse 650
Nice 516
GEORGIA
Tbilisi 1,300
GERMANY
Berlin 3,470
Hamburg 1,706
Munich 1,240
Cologne 964
Frankfurt 651
Essen 616
Dortmund 600
Stuttgart 587
Düsseldorf 571
Bremen 549
Duisburg 535
Hanover 524
GHANA
Accra 949
GREECE
Athens 3,097
GUATEMALA
Guatemala 1,167
GUINEA
Conakry 1,508
HAITI
Port-au-Prince 1,255
HONDURAS
Tegucigalpa 813
HUNGARY
Budapest 1,885
INDIA
Bombay (Mumbai) 12,572
Calcutta (Kolkata) 10,916
Delhi 7,207
Madras (Chennai) 5,361
Hyderabad 4,280
Bangalore 4,087
Ahmadabad 3,298
Pune 2,485
Kanpur 2,111
Nagpur 1,661
Lucknow 1,642
Surat 1,517
Jaipur 1,514
Coimbatore 1,136
Vadodara 1,115
Indore 1,104
Patna 1,099
Madurai 1,094
Bhopal 1,064
Vishakhapatnam 1,052
Varanasi 1,026
Ludhiana 1,012
INDONESIA
Jakarta 11,500
Surabaya 2,701
Bandung 2,368
Medan 1,910
Semarang 1,366
Palembang 1,352
Tangerang 1,198
Ujung Pandang 1,092
Bandar Lampung 832
Malang 763
Padang 721
Pakanbaru 558
Samarinda 536
Banjarmasin 535
Surakarta 516
IRAN
Tehran 6,750
Mashhad 1,964
Esfahan 1,221
Tabriz 1,166
Shiraz 1,043
Ahvaz 828
Qom 780
Bakhtaran 666
Karaj 588
IRAQ
Baghdad 3,841
Diyala 961
As Sulaymaniyah 952
Arbil 770
Al Mawsil 664
Kadhimain 521
IRELAND
Dublin 952
ISRAEL
Tel Aviv-Yafo 1,502
Jerusalem 591
ITALY
Rome 2,775
Milan 1,369
Naples 1,067
Turin 962
Palermo 698
Genoa 678
IVORY COAST (CÔTE D'IVOIRE)
Abidjan 2,500
JAMAICA
Kingston 644
JAPAN
Tokyo-Yokohama 26,836
Osaka 10,601
Nagoya 2,152
Sapporo 1,757
Kyoto 1,464
Kobe 1,424
Fukuoka 1,285
Kawasaki 1,203
Hiroshima 1,109
Kitakyushu 1,020
Sendai 971
Chiba 857
Sakai 803
Kumamoto 650
Okayama 616
Sagamihara 571
Hamamatsu 562
Kagoshima 546
Funabashi 541
Higashiosaka 517
Hachioji 503
JORDAN
Amman 1,300
Az-Zarqā 609
KAZAKSTAN
Almaty 1,150
Qaraghandy 573
KENYA
Nairobi 2,000
Mombasa 600
KOREA, NORTH
Pyŏngyang 2,639
Hamhung 775
Chŏngjin 754
Chinnampo 691
Sinŭiju 500
KOREA, SOUTH
Seoul 11,641
Pusan 3,814
Taegu 2,449
Inchon 2,308
Taejŏn 1,272
Kwangju 1,258
Ulsan 967
Sŏngnam 869
Puch'on 779
Suwŏn 756
Anyang 590
Chŏnju 563
Chŏngju 531
Ansan 510
P'ohang 509
KYRGYZSTAN
Bishkek 584
LATVIA
Riga 846
LEBANON
Beirut 1,900
Tripoli 500
LIBYA
Tripoli 1,083
LITHUANIA
Vilnius 580
MACEDONIA
Skopje 541
MADAGASCAR
Antananarivo 1,053
MALAYSIA
Kuala Lumpur 1,145
MALI
Bamako 800
MAURITANIA
Nouakchott 735
MEXICO
Mexico City 15,048
Guadalajara 2,847
Monterrey 2,522
Puebla 1,055
León 872
Ciudad Juárez 798
Tijuana 743
Culiacán Rosales 602
Mexicali 602
Acapulco de Juárez 592
Mérida 557
Chihuahua 530
San Luis Potosí 526
Aguascalientés 506
MOLDOVA
Chişinău 700
MONGOLIA
Ulan Bator 627
MOROCCO
Casablanca 3,079
Rabat-Salé 1,344
Fès 735
Marrakesh 621
MOZAMBIQUE
Maputo 2,000
NEPAL
Katmandu 535
NETHERLANDS
Amsterdam 1,101
Rotterdam 1,076
The Hague 694
Utrecht 548
NEW ZEALAND
Auckland 997
NICARAGUA
Managua 864
NIGERIA
Lagos 10,287
Ibadan 1,365
Ogbomosho 712
Kano 657
NORWAY
Oslo 714
PAKISTAN
Karachi 9,863
Lahore 5,085
Faisalabad 1,875
Peshawar 1,676
Gujranwala 1,663
Rawalpindi 1,290
Multan 1,257
Hyderabad 1,107
PARAGUAY
Asunción 945
PERU
Lima-Callao 6,601
Callao 638
Arequipa 620
Trujillo 509
PHILIPPINES
Manila 9,280
Quezon City 1,989
Davao 1,191
Caloocan 1,023
Cebu 662
Zamboanga 511
POLAND
Warsaw 1,638
Lódz 825
Kraków 745
Wroclaw 642
Poznań 581
PORTUGAL
Lisbon 2,561
Oporto 1,174
ROMANIA
Bucharest 2,060
RUSSIA
Moscow 9,233
St Petersburg 4,883
Nizhniy Novgorod 1,425
Novosibirsk 1,400
Yekaterinburg 1,300
Samara 1,200
Omsk 1,200
Chelyabinsk 1,100
Kazan 1,100
Ufa 1,100
Volgograd 1,003
Perm 1,000
Rostov 1,000
Voronezh 908
Saratov 895
Krasnoyarsk 869
Togliatti 689
Simbirsk 678
Izhevsk 654
Krasnodar 645
Vladivostok 632
Yaroslavl 629
Khabarovsk 618
Barnaul 596
Irkutsk 585
Novokuznetsk 572
Ryazan 536
Penza 534
Orenburg 532
Tula 532
Naberezhnyye-Chelny 526
Kemerovo 503
SAUDI ARABIA
Riyadh 1,800
Jedda 1,500
Mecca 630
SENEGAL
Dakar 1,571
SIERRA LEONE
Freetown 505
SINGAPORE
Singapore 3,104
SOMALIA
Mogadishu 1,000
SOUTH AFRICA
Cape Town 2,350
East Rand 1,379
Johannesburg 1,196
Durban 1,137
Pretoria 1,080
West Rand 870
Port Elizabeth 853
Vanderbijlpark-Vereeniging 774
Soweto 597
Sasolburg 540
SPAIN
Madrid 3,029
Barcelona 1,614
Valencia 763
Sevilla 719
Zaragoza 607
Málaga 532
SRI LANKA
Colombo 1,863
SUDAN
Omdurman 1,267
Khartoum 925
Khartoum North 879
SWEDEN
Stockholm 1,744
Göteborg 775
SWITZERLAND
Zürich 1,175
Bern 942
SYRIA
Aleppo 1,591
Damascus 1,549
Homs 644
TAIWAN
Taipei 2,653
Kaohsiung 1,405
Taichung 817
Tainan 700
Panchiao 544
TAJIKISTAN
Dushanbe 524
TANZANIA
Dar-es-Salaam 1,361
THAILAND
Bangkok 5,572
TOGO
Lomé 590
TUNISIA
Tunis 1,827
TURKEY
Istanbul 7,490
Ankara 3,028
Izmir 2,333
Adana 1,472
Bursa 1,317
Konya 1,040
Gaziantep 930
Icel 908
Antalya 734
Diyarbakir 677
Kocaeli 661
Urfa 649
Kayseri 648
Manisa 641
Hatay 561
Samsun 557
Eskisehir 508
Balikesir 501
TURKMENISTAN
Ashkhabad 536
UGANDA
Kampala 773
UKRAINE
Kiev 2,630
Kharkiv 1,555
Dnipropetrovsk 1,147
Donetsk 1,088
Odesa 1,046
Zaporizhzhya 887
Lviv 802
Kryyyy Rih 720
Mariupol 510
Mykolayiv 508
UNITED KINGDOM
London 8,089
Birmingham 2,373
Manchester 2,353
Liverpool 852
Glasgow 832
Sheffield 661
Nottingham 649
Newcastle 617
Bristol 552
Leeds 529
UNITED STATES
New York 16,329
Los Angeles 12,410
Chicago 7,668
Philadelphia 4,949
Washington, DC 4,466
Detroit 4,307
Houston 3,653
Atlanta 3,331
Boston 3,240
Dallas 2,898
Minneapolis-St Paul 2,688
San Diego 2,632
St Louis 2,536
Phoenix 2,473
Baltimore 2,458
Pittsburgh 2,402
Cleveland 2,222
San Francisco 2,182
Seattle 2,180
Tampa 2,157
Miami 2,025
Newark 1,934
Denver 1,796
Portland (Or.) 1,676
Kansas City (Mo.) 1,647
Cincinnati 1,581
San Jose 1,557
Norfolk 1,529
Indianapolis 1,462
Milwaukee 1,456
Sacramento 1,441
San Antonio 1,437
Columbus (Oh.) 1,423
New Orleans 1,309
Charlotte 1,260
Buffalo 1,189
Salt Lake City 1,178
Hartford 1,151
Oklahoma 1,007
Jacksonville (Fl.) 665
Omaha 663
Memphis 614
El Paso 579
Austin 514
Nashville 505
URUGUAY
Montevideo 1,378
UZBEKISTAN
Tashkent 2,107
VENEZUELA
Caracas 2,784
Maracaibo 1,364
Valencia 1,032
Maracay 800
Barquisimeto 745
Ciudad Guayana 524
VIETNAM
Ho Chi Minh City 4,322
Hanoi 3,056
Haiphong 783
YEMEN
Sana 972
Aden 562
YUGOSLAVIA
Belgrade 1,137
ZAMBIA
Lusaka 982
ZIMBABWE
Harare 1,189
Bulawayo 622

* SAR = Special Administrative Region of China

GENERAL REFERENCE

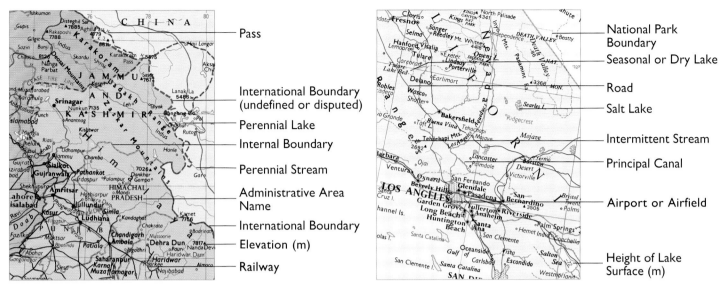

Pass

International Boundary (undefined or disputed)

Perennial Lake

Internal Boundary

Perennial Stream

Administrative Area Name

International Boundary

Elevation (m)

Railway

National Park Boundary

Seasonal or Dry Lake

Road

Salt Lake

Intermittent Stream

Principal Canal

Airport or Airfield

Height of Lake Surface (m)

Settlements

Settlement symbols and type styles vary according to the scale of each map and indicate the importance of towns rather than specific population figures.

TIME ZONES

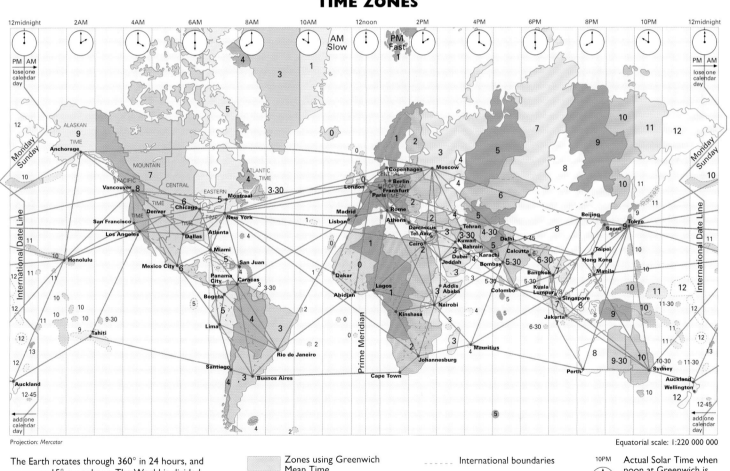

Projection: *Mercator*

Equatorial scale: 1:220 000 000

The Earth rotates through 360° in 24 hours, and so moves 15° every hour. The World is divided into 24 standard time zones, each centred on lines of longitude at 15° intervals.

The Greenwich meridian lies on the centre of the first zone. All places to the west of Greenwich are one hour behind for every 15° of longitude; places to the east are ahead by one hour for every 15°.

Zones using Greenwich Mean Time	
Half hour zones	
Zones fast of Greenwich Mean Time	
Zones slow of Greenwich Mean Time	

International boundaries

Time zone boundaries

International date line

Selected air routes

10PM Actual Solar Time when noon at Greenwich is shown along the top of the map.

Note: Certain of the time zones are affected by the incidence of "Summer Time" in countries where it is adopted.

CARTOGRAPHY BY PHILIP'S.

Projection: Hammer Equal Area

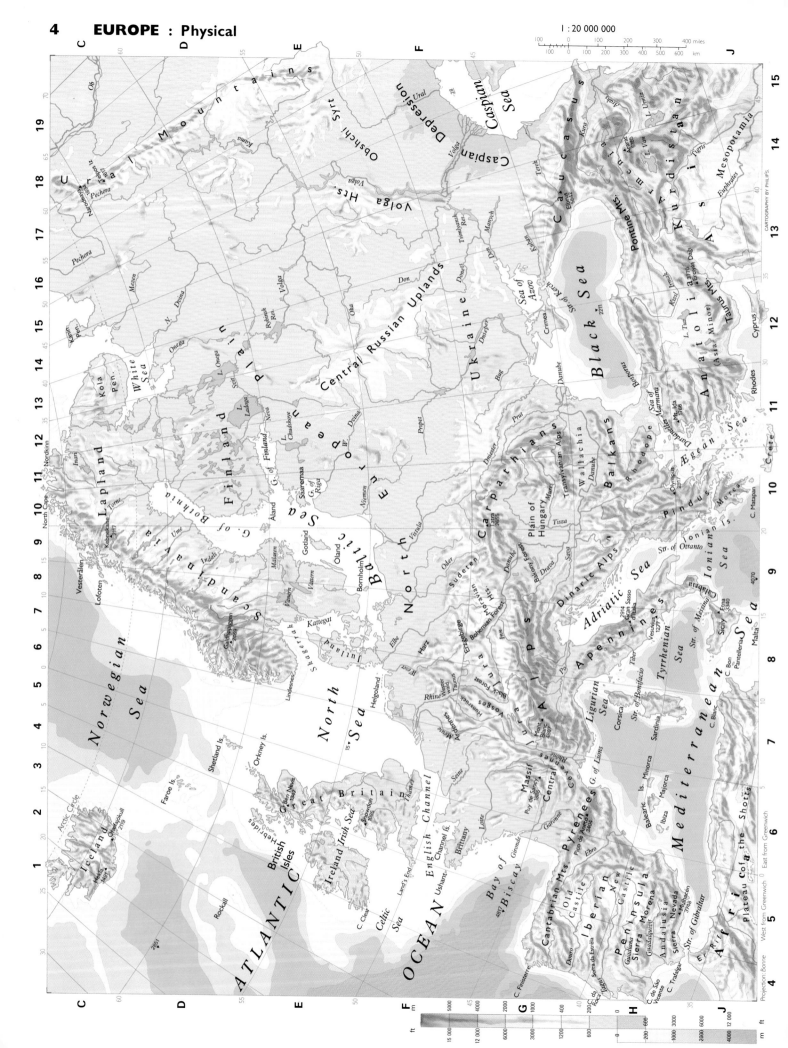

1 : 20 000 000

CARTOGRAPHY BY PHILIP'S

Projection: Bonne

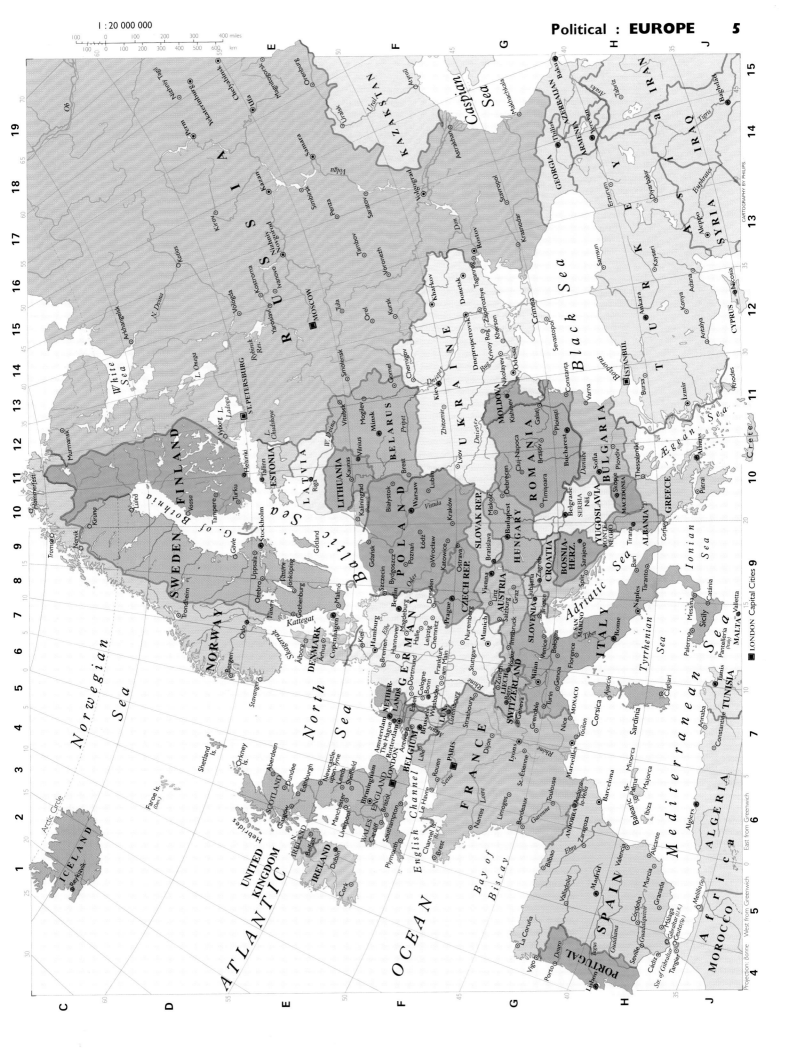

1 : 10 000 000

ICELAND
On the same scale   West from Greenwich 18

Projection: Conical with two standard parallels

East from Greenwich

COPYRIGHT. GEORGE PHILIP & SON. LTD.

1 : 5 000 000

Projection: Conical with two standard parallels

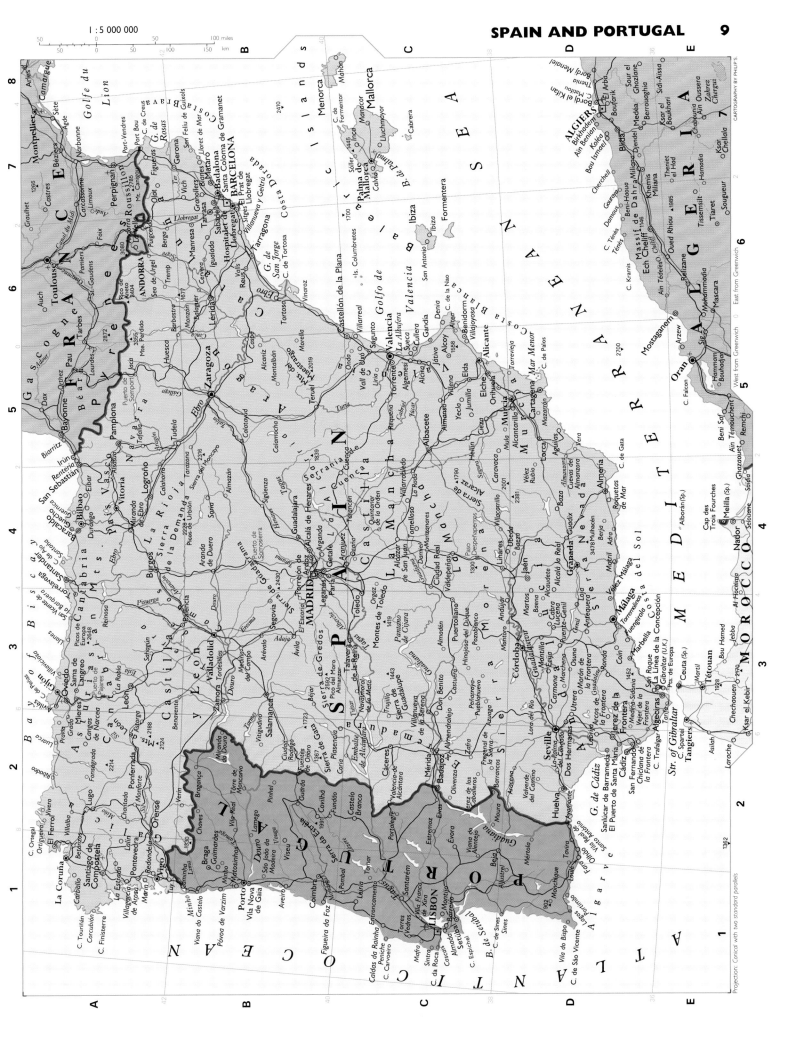

Projection: Conical with two standard parallels

1 : 5 000 000

50 0 50 100 miles
0 50 100 150 km

East from Greenwich

CARTOGRAPHY BY PHILIP'S

LITHUANIA

BELARUS

POLAND

UKRAINE

SLOVAK REP.

CZECH REP.

HUNGARY

ROMANIA

MOLDOVA

YUGOSLAVIA

BULGARIA

BOSNIA-HERZEGOVINA

CROATIA

Kaliningrad (Russia)

Vilnius · MINSK · Mogilev · Krychaw · Mstsislaw · Shklow · Borisov · Krupki · Slawharad · Bykhaw · Cherykaw

Gdańsk · Gdynia · Sopot · Gdynia · Wejherowo · Rumia · Lębork · Bytów · Starogard Gdański · Tczew · Elbląg · Malbork · Kwidzyn · Iława · Braniewo · Bagrationovsk · Gvardeysk · Chernyakhovsk · Gusev

WARSAW · Łódź · Wrocław · Kraków · Katowice · Gliwice · Bytom · Sosnowiec · Chorzów · Tychy · Zabrze

Grodno · Baranovichi · Slutsk · Bobruysk · Gomel · Dobrush · Zhlobin · Rechytsa · Svyetlahorsk · Salihorsk

Pinsk · Brest · Kobryn · Mazyr · Khoyniki · Chernobyl

KIEV · Zhitomir · Rovno · Lutsk · Lvov · Ternopol · Khmelnitskiy · Vinnitsa · Chernovtsy

Ivano-Frankovsk · Uzhhorod · Mukachevo · Kolomyya

BUDAPEST · Debrecen · Miskolc · Szeged · Pécs · Győr

BRATISLAVA · Košice · Nitra

Cluj-Napoca · Oradea · Timișoara · Arad · Sibiu · Brașov · Ploiești · BUCHAREST · Craiova · Galați · Brăila · Constanța · Bacău · Iași · Piatra Neamț · Suceava · Botoșani · Baia Mare · Satu Mare · Târgu Mureș

KISHINEV · Tiraspol · Tighina · Beltsy · Orhei · Cahul

BELGRADE · Novi Sad · Subotica

SARAJEVO · Tuzla · Zenica · Banja Luka · Doboj

Masurian Lakes · Pripet Marshes · Carpathians · Transylvania · Transylvanian Alps · Wallachia · Moldavia · Bessarabia · Dobruja · Vojvodina

Vistula · Danube · Dniester · Drava · Sava · Tisza · Prut · Siret · Mureș

Projection: Conical with two standard parallels

Khalmer-Yu 1363
Vorkuta
Labytnangi
Salekhard
Berezovo
Sosva
Ivdel
Sos'va
Serov
Krasnoturinsk
Nizhniy Tagil
YEKATERINBURG (Sverdlovsk)
Perkouralsk
Ufa
Miass
Zlatoust
Belofetsk
Novotroitsk
Orsk

U R A L
M O U N T A I N S
Narodnaya 1894
Tel'pos Iz 1617
Intu
Usa
Tisa
Pechora
Troitsko-Pechorsk
Kama
Chusovoy
Lys'va
PERM
Kizel
Berezniki
Solikamsk 1569
Kungur
Yaman-Tau 1640
Nyazepetrovsk
Chernikovsk
BASHKORTOSTAN
Sterlitamak
Salovat
Magnitogorsk
Kumertau
Orenburg
Sorochinsk

I Z M A
Arctic Circle
Ust' Usa
Bol'shezemel'sk
Tundra
Pechora
Usa

Kolguyev
Kanin Pen.
G. of Pechora
Naryan-Mar
Malozemel'sk Tundra
Ust' Tsilma
Ukhta
Zheleznodorozhny
Sosnogorsk
Pechora
463
Vychegda
Syktyvkar
Koslan
Glazov 337
UDMURTIA
Votkinsk
Izhevsk
Sarapul
Naberezhnyye Chelny
Mukhi
Slobodskoy
Nolinsk
Vyatka
KAZAN
TATARSTAN
Bugulma
Buguruslan
Buzuluk

Yb
Pinyug
Kirov
Kotelnich
Sharya
Shakhunya
Velluga
MARI EL
Yoshkar Ola
Cheboksary
CHUVASHIA
Alatyr
Simbirsk
Syzran
Kuznetsk 351
Volga
Balakovo

Kanin Nos
Chesha B.
Mezen
Karpogory
Pinega
Kotlas
Totma
Sukhona
Vetluga
Neya
Gorki Reservoir
Dzerzhinsk
Arzamas
MORDVINIA
Saransk
Penza
Khopor
Serdobsk

Rybachi Pen.
Kola B.
Murmansk
1191
Monchegorsk
Imandra
Kirovsk
Kola Pen.
Ponoy
Kandalaksha G.
White Sea
Dvina B.
Severodvinsk
Arkhangelsk
Onega
Onega
Plesetsk
Nyandoma
Vel'sk
Kharovsk
Vologda
Gryazovets
Bui
Kostroma
Kineshma
Ivanovo
Nizhniy Novgorod
Vladimir
Murom
Orekhovo-Zuyevo
Ryazan
Novomoskovsk
Michurinsk
Lipetsk
Tambov
Morshansk
Yelets

Pedenga
Kandalaksha
Pya L.
Kuito L.
Top L.
Kem
Belomorsk
Medvezhyegorsk
KARELIA
417 Sg.
Povenets
Kargopol'
Vytegra
Beloye L.
Belozersk
Cherepovets
Rybinsk Reservoir
Rybinsk
Yaroslavl
Rostov
Kimry
Sergiyev Posad
MOSCOW
Podolsk
Serpukhov
Kaluga
Tula 293
Orel
Bryansk

L. Tuari
Lapland
Monchegorsk
Kem
Kuit L.
Segozero
Medvezhyegorsk
Segezha
Podporozhye
Olonets
Petrozavodsk
L. Onega
Svir
Lodeynoye Pole
Novaya Ladoga
L. Ladoga
Volkhov
Tikhvin
Borovichi
Vyshniy Volochek 343
Tver
Rzhev
Vyazma
Smolensk
Roslavl

N O R W A Y
Laplalid
Napuk
2117
Kebnekaise
Gällivare
Kiruna
Torne L.
Torne
Muonio
Kemijärvi
Kemi
Rovaniemi
Torne
Kalix
Luleå
Kemi
Oulu
F I N L A N D
Kuopio
Savonlinna
Sortavala
Priozersk
St. Petersburg
Leningrad
Novgorod
L. Ilmen
Staraya Russa
Velikiye Luki
Ostrov
Opochka

S W E D E N
Umeå
Angerman
Sundsvall
Soderhamn
Gulf of Bothnia
Vaasa
Pori
Tampere
Turku
Helsinki
Kotka
Vyborg
G. of Finland
Tallinn
ESTONIA
Narva
Chudskoye L.
Pskov
Velikaya
LATVIA
Valga
Pärnu
Riga
G. of Riga
Jelgava
Daugavpils
Daugava
Polotsk
Vitebsk
Orsha
Mogilev
Gomel

Åland Is. (Ahvenanmaa)
Stockholm
Hiiumaa
Saaremaa
Ventspils
Liepaja
Klaipeda
Soveltsk
Kaliningrad
RUSSIA
LITHUANIA
228
Šiauliai
Kaunas
Vilnius
Grodno
Białystok
Brest
MINSK
BELARUS
Borisov
Berezina
Baranovichi
Bobruysk
346
Pinsk
Pripet
Marshes
Pripet
Gorom
Chernigov
Kiev

WARSAW
POLAND
Lublin

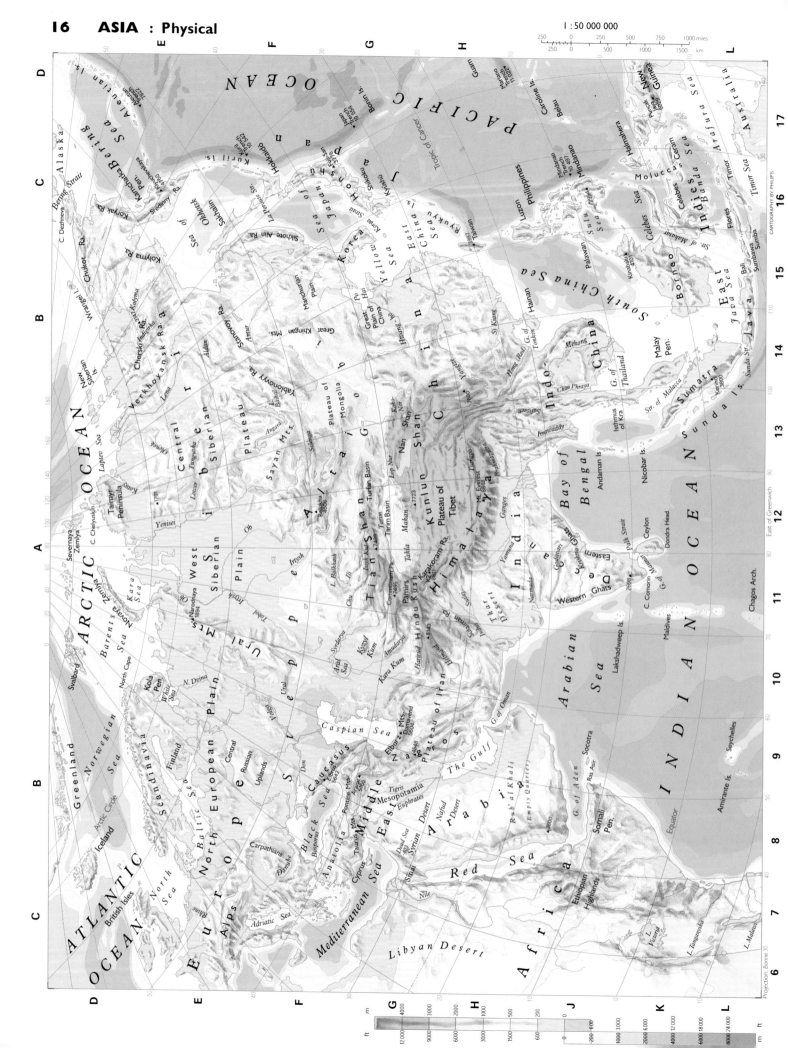

1 : 50 000 000

CARTOGRAPHY BY PHILIPS

Projection: Bonne

East of Greenwich

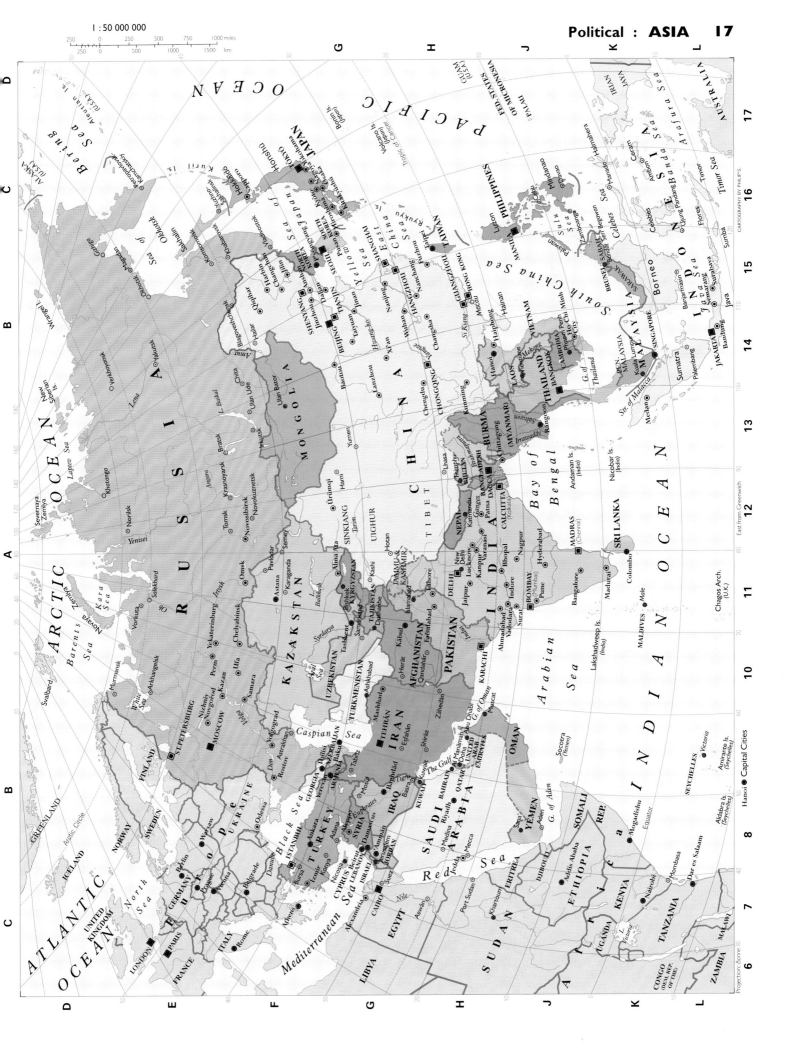

1 : 35 000 000

```
200        400    600   800 miles
400    0        400    800   1200 km
```

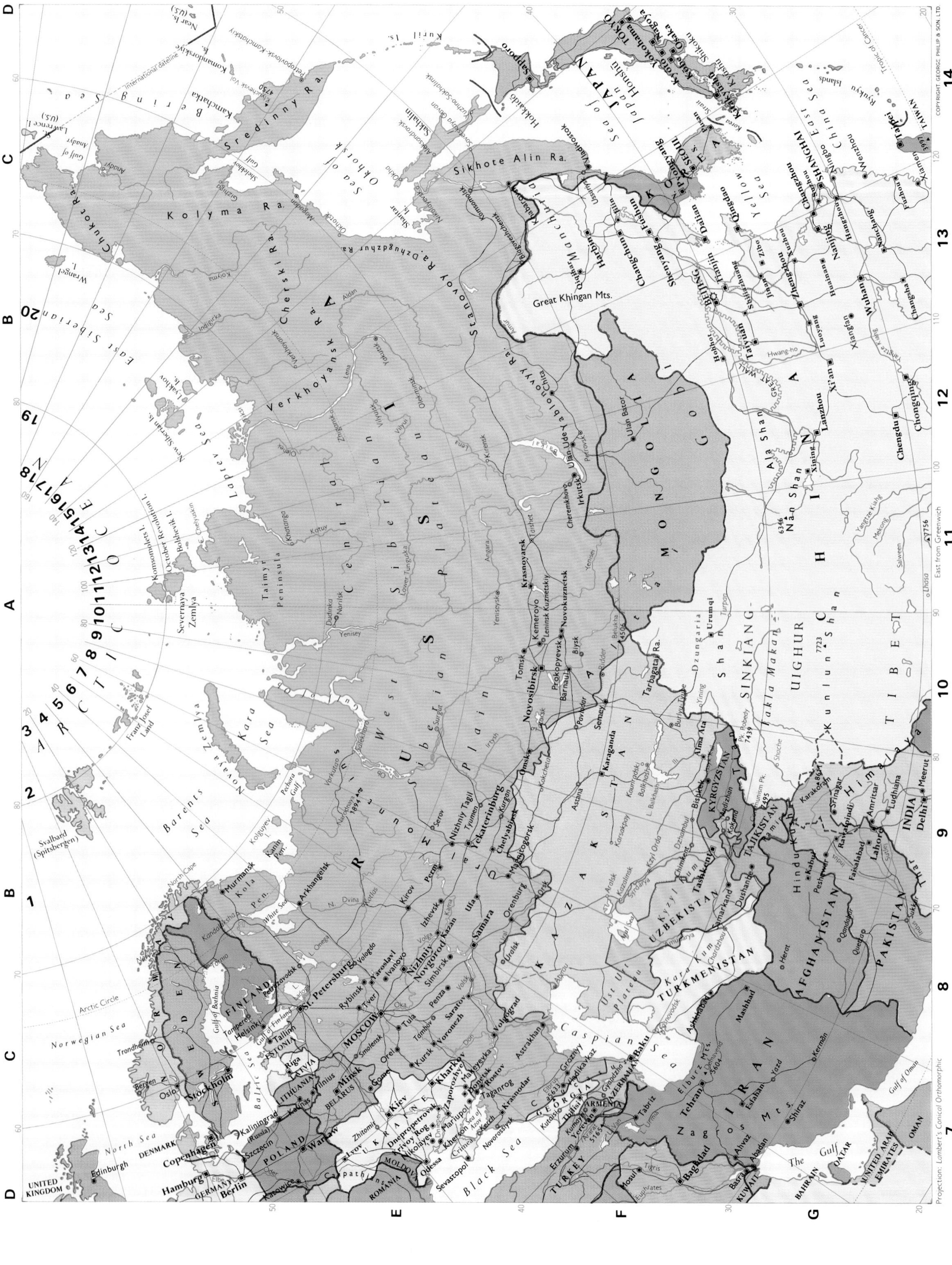

COPYRIGHT GEORGE PHILIP & SON, LTD.

Projection: Lambert's Conical Orthomorphic

Major labels visible on the map include:

RUSSIA, KAZAKSTAN, MONGOLIA, CHINA, SINKIANG-UIGHUR, TIBET, INDIA, PAKISTAN, AFGHANISTAN, IRAN, TURKMENISTAN, UZBEKISTAN, TAJIKISTAN, KYRGYZSTAN, TURKEY, GEORGIA, ARMENIA, AZERBAIJAN, UKRAINE, BELARUS, POLAND, ROMANIA, MOLDOVA, GERMANY, DENMARK, SWEDEN, NORWAY, FINLAND, ESTONIA, LATVIA, LITHUANIA, UNITED KINGDOM, JAPAN, KOREA, TAIWAN, KUWAIT, BAHRAIN, QATAR, UNITED ARAB EMIRATES, OMAN

MOSCOW, St. Petersburg, Kiev, Minsk, Warsaw, Berlin, Hamburg, Copenhagen, Oslo, Stockholm, Helsinki, Tallinn, Riga, Vilnius, Kaliningrad, Murmansk, Arkhangelsk, Kirov, Perm, Ekaterinburg, Chelyabinsk, Omsk, Novosibirsk, Krasnoyarsk, Irkutsk, Ulan Ude, Ulan Bator, Vladivostok, Khabarovsk, Komsomolsk, Kamchatka, Anadyr, BEIJING, SHANGHAI, Tianjin, Wuhan, Chengdu, Chongqing, Lanzhou, Urumqi, Lhasa, Delhi, Amritsar, Lahore, Rawalpindi, Kabul, Kandahar, Herat, Mashhad, Tehran, Tabriz, Baghdad, Basra, Kuwait, Abadan, Shiraz, Baku, Tbilisi, Yerevan, Ankara, Erzurum

Seas and features: Bering Sea, Sea of Okhotsk, Sea of Japan, Yellow Sea, East China Sea, Kara Sea, Barents Sea, Laptev Sea, East Siberian Sea, Baltic Sea, North Sea, Norwegian Sea, Black Sea, Caspian Sea, The Gulf, Gulf of Oman, Arctic Circle, Tropic of Cancer

Physical: Kolyma Ra., Chersky Ra., Verkhoyansk Ra., Stanovoy Ra., Sikhote Alin Ra., Central Siberian Plateau, West Siberian Plain, Ural Mts., Great Khingan Mts., Himalaya, Hindu Kush, Zagros Mts., Elburz Mts., Kunlun Shan, Tien Shan, Nan Shan, Ala Shan, Takla Makan, Gobi, Taimyr Peninsula, Kamchatka, Sakhalin, Kuril Is., Novaya Zemlya, Severnaya Zemlya, Franz Josef Land, Svalbard (Spitsbergen), Wrangel I.

Rivers: Lena, Ob, Yenisey, Volga, Amur, Angara, Hwang-ho, Yangtze Kiang, Don, Dnieper

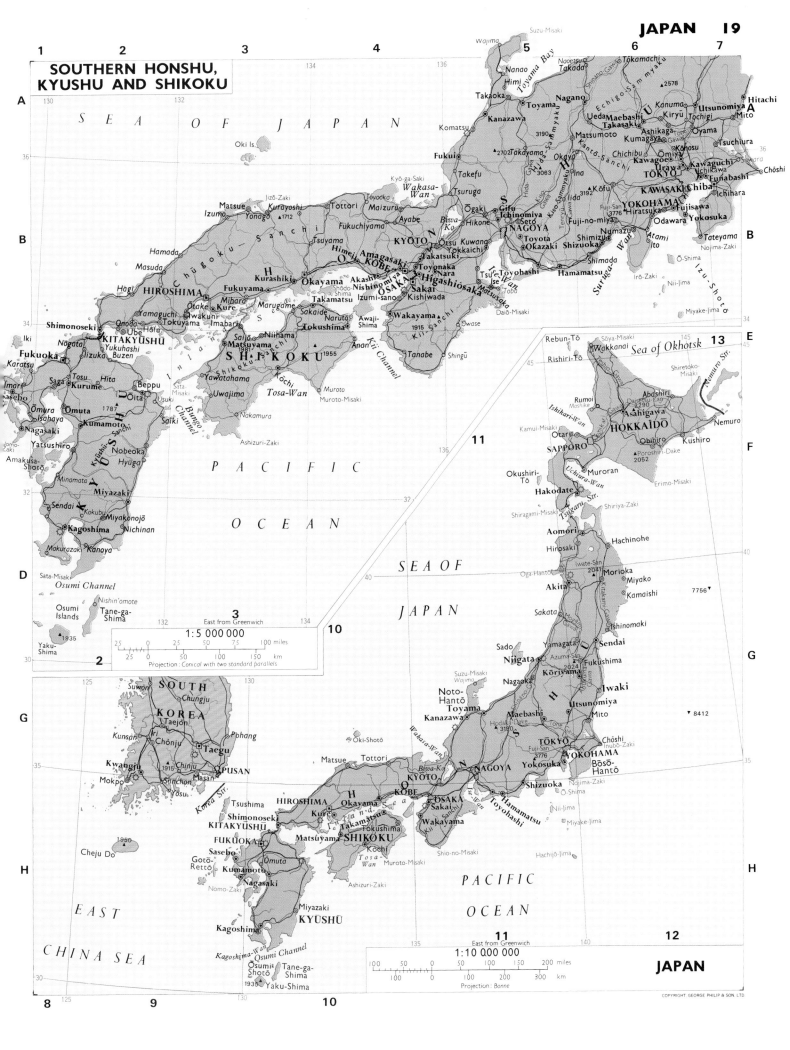

1 2 3 4 5

KAZAKSTAN

RUSSIA

Karaganda
Karsakpay
Karkaralinsk
Semey
Öskeman
Rubtsovsk
Sayah
Western
Angarsk
Cheremkhovo
Irkutsk
455
Munku Sardyk 3491
Khuakem
Tannu Ola
Uvs Nuur
Treryn Gol
Hatgal
Hövsgöl Nuur
Selenge
Morön
Aftanbul
Belukha 4506
Zyryanovsk
1565
Ayoguz
Lake Zaisan
Ulaangom
Hyargas Nuur
Orhon Gol
342
Lake Balkhash
Taldy-Kurgan
Tarbagatai Ra.
Tacheng
Altay
Fuyun
Har Us Nuur
Hovd
Döröö Nuur
Ulyasutay
Khangai
MONGO
Ala Tau
Ala Kul
Fuhai
4362
Tsetserleg
Ulan Bator
Dzzungarian Gates
Ulungur
Altai
Dzumod
Bishkek
Dzhambul
Issyk-Kul
Alma Ata
Yining
Bole
Usu
Qitai
Buyanhongor
KYRGYZSTAN
1609
Namangan
Andizhan
Naryn
Tien
Ili
Dzungaria
Shan
Ürümqi
5445
Turpan
154
4925
Hami
Dalandzadgad
Go
Rik Pobedy 7439
Kuqa
UIGHUR
Bosten (Bagrax) Hu
Korla
Kuruktag
Gaxun Nur
Kashi
Aksu
SINKIANG
Tarim He
Tarim Basin
Lop Nor
Dunhuang
Anxi
Linhe
Shache
Takla Makan
Ruoqiang
Altun Shan
Yumen
Jiayuguan
Ala Shan
Wuhai
2514
1635
Yecheng
Hotan
Yutian
Qiemo
6346
Zhangye
Alxa Zuoqi
NINGXIA
Yinchuan HUIZU
Mu
Karakoram K 8611
Karakoram Pass 5575
7723
Kun-lun
Shan
Da Qaidam
Qaidam pendi
Golmud
Tianjun
Qinghai Hu 3205
Dulan
Gonghe
Xining
Wuwei
ZIZHIQU
Wuzhong
8126
JAMMU & KASHMIR
Srinagar
Leh
Rutog
Gar
TIBET
Ngoring Hu 4237
Gyaring Hu
Maqen
6094
Min Xian
Linxia
Pingliang
Baoji
LANZHOU
Tianshui
S
Nanda Devi 7817
Buran
Mapam Yumco
Tangha Range
Amdo
Nagqu
Yushu
Yalong
Bayan Har Shan
Da Xue Shan
Garze
Min
Wudu
Hanzhong
4113
C
H
Dehra Dun
Zhongba
Xainza
Siling Co 4495
Nam Co 4627
Qamdo
Mekong
Ninging Shan
Shaluli
Shan
Daliang Shan
Mianyang
Daxian
Meerut
Moradabad
DELHI
Bareilly
Aligarh
Agra
NEPAL
Dhaulagiri 8221
Ghaghra
Nyenchen Tanglha Range
Lhasa
Yarlung Zangbo
Xigaze
Namcha Barwa 7756
Bomi
Gogga Shan 7600
Xichang
Zhongdian
CHENGDU
Nanchong
Hechuan
Neijiang
SICHUAN
KANPUR
Gwalior
LUCKNOW
Katmandu
Gorakhpur
Everest 8848
Lhazê
Yamzho Yumco
Zayu
Na Jiang
5881
Lijiang
Wutongqiao
Zigong
Luzhou
CHONGQ
INDIA
Jhansi
Allahabad
Patna
Varanasi
BHUTAN
Thimphu
Dibrugarh
Brahmaputra
Tezpur
Parkai Hills
3411
Zhongdian
Daili Shan
Zhaotong
Yibin
Zunyi
GUIZHO
Jabalpur
Agra
Koch Bihar
Gauhati
Khasi Hills
Myitkyina
Xiaguan
Dongchuan
Zhanyi
Guiyang
Anshun
Duyun
Rajshahi
BANGLADESH
Imphal 382
Silchar
Bhamo
Luxi
Baoshan
KUNMING
Xingyi
Hechi
GUA
Ranchi
Jamshedpur
Haora
Khulna
DACCA (Dhaka)
Narayangaj
CHITTAGONG
Monywa
BURMA (MYANMAR)
Mandalay
2650
YUNNAN
Shiping
Gejiu
Wenshan
Hongshui
Bose
ZHU
Nanning
ZIZ
NAGPUR
Raipur
Cuttack
Mahanadi
CALCUTTA (Kolkata)
Arakan Yoma
Victoria 3053
Pegu Yoma
Irrawaddy
3143
Song Da (Black)
Pingxiang
VIETNAM
Qinzhou
Warangal
BAY OF
BENGAL
Akyab
Yamethin
Toungoo
2763 THAILAND
Sittang
Salween
Mekong
Luang Prabang
LAOS
Hoa-binh
HANOI
HAIPHONG
Gulf of
Tonkin
Vishakhapatnam

Tropic of Cancer

50

40

30

20

B

C

D

E

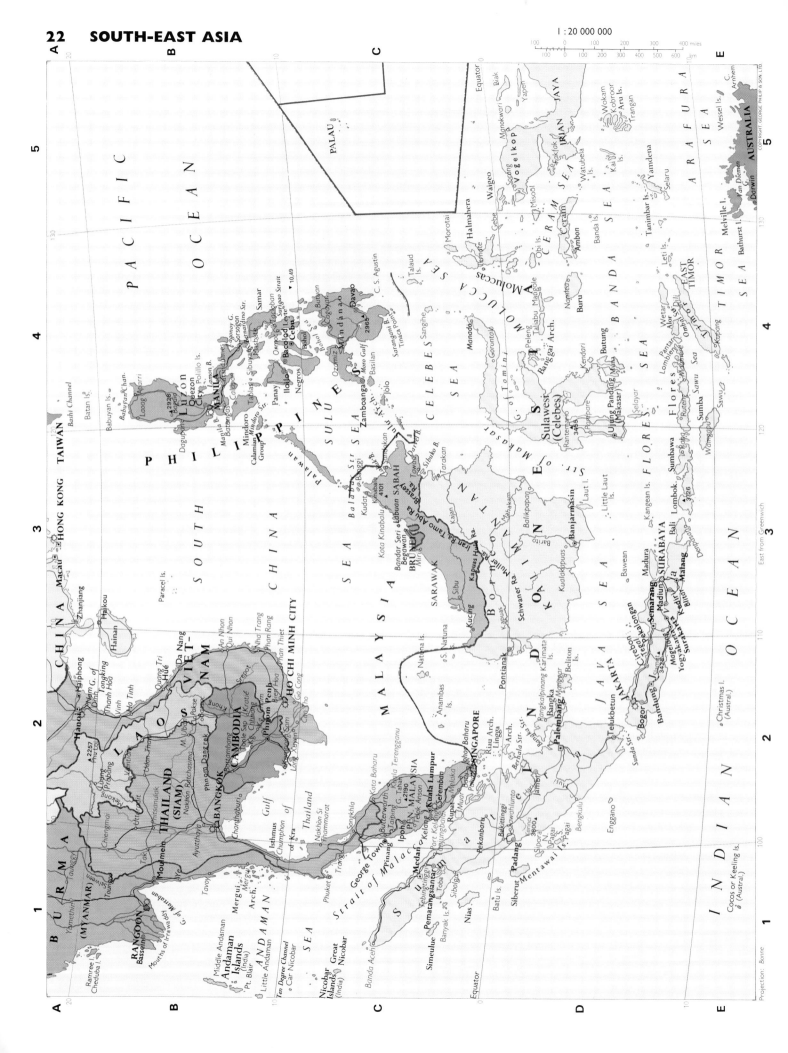

1 : 20 000 000

PACIFIC OCEAN

CHINA

TAIWAN

HONG KONG

Macau

Zhanjiang

Haikou

Hainan

Paracel Is.

BURMA (MYANMAR)

Mandalay

Taunggyi

Chiengmai

Phitsanulok

Uttaradit

THAILAND (SIAM)

BANGKOK

Ayutthaya

Nakhon Ratchasima

Chanthaburi

LAOS

Vientiane

Udon Thani

Luang Prabang

Mekong

Phnom Dangrek

CAMBODIA

Battambang

Tonle Sap

Kampong Cham

Phnom Penh

VIET-NAM

Hanoi

Haiphong

Thanh Hoa

Vinh

Quang Tri

Hué

Da Nang

An Nhon

Qui Nhon

Nha Trang

Phan Rang

Phan Thiet

HO CHI MINH CITY

SOUTH CHINA SEA

PHILIPPINES

Luzon

MANILA

Quezon City

Baguio

Laoag

Babuyan Is.

Batan Is.

Babuyan Chan.

Bashi Channel

Batan Is.

Mindoro

Calamian Group

Panay

Negros

Bacolod

Cebu

Bohol

Samar

Masbate

Leyte

Surigao Strait

Mindanao

Davao

Zamboanga

Basilan

Jolo

SULU SEA

Palawan

BRUNEI

Bandar Seri Begawan

SARAWAK

Kuching

SABAH

Kota Kinabalu

MALAYSIA

PEN. MALAYSIA

Kuala Lumpur

Seremban

Ipoh

George Town

Penang

SINGAPORE

Johor Baharu

Kota Bharu

Kuala Terengganu

CELEBES SEA

Manado

Gorontalo

SULAWESI (Celebes)

Ujung Pandang (Makasar)

Str. of Makasar

KALIMANTAN

Balikpapan

Banjarmasin

Pontianak

BORNEO

INDONESIA

Palembang

Jambi

JAKARTA

Bogor

Bandung

Cirebon

Semarang

SURABAYA

Madura

JAVA SEA

Bali

Lombok

Sumbawa

FLORES SEA

Flores

Sumba

Timor

EAST TIMOR

BANDA SEA

CERAM SEA

Moluccas

IRIAN JAYA

ARAFURA SEA

AUSTRALIA

Darwin

INDIAN OCEAN

ANDAMAN SEA

Andaman Islands (India)

Nicobar Islands (India)

Equator

East from Greenwich

Projection: Bonne

COPYRIGHT GEORGE PHILIP & SON LTD.

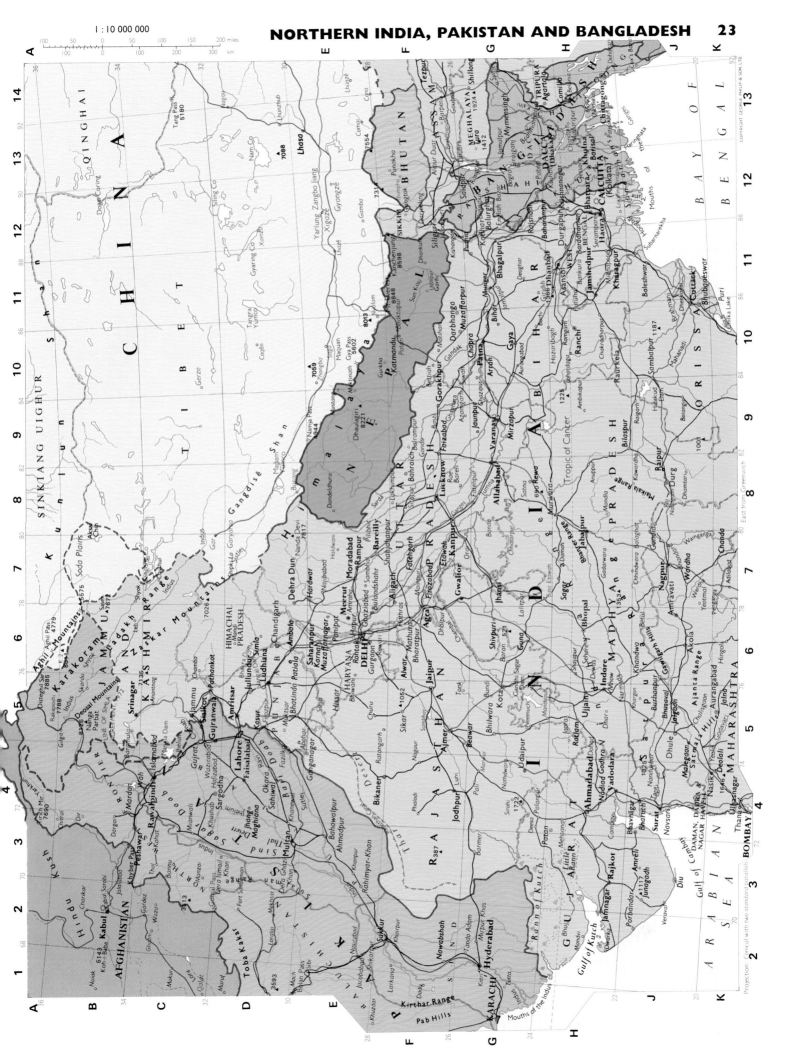

1 : 10 000 000

1 2 3 4 5

B

TURKEY
Konya Kayseri Malatya Erzurum Yerevan Gyandzha
Mersin Adana Gaziantep Diyarbakir **AZERBAIJAN** Baku
Nicosia **CYPRUS** Antakya
LEBANON Latakia Aleppo (Halab) Mosul Urmia Tabriz Ardabil Lenkoran
Tripoli Hama Erbil Zanjan Rasht Anzali Babol **Caspian Sea**
Beirut **SYRIA** Homs Euphrates Kirkuk Qazvin Elburz Mountains Krasnovodsk
Alexandria Haifa Damascus **IRAQ** Bakhtaran Hamadan Tehran Mashhad **Kara Bogaz Gol**
Damanhur Tel Aviv- Ar Ramadi Karbala Baghdad Qom Demavend 5604 **TURKMENISTAN**
Mansura Jaffa Amman Hilla Al km Araq Kashan Ashkhabad Urgench **UZBEKISTAN**
Dumyat **ISRAEL** Jerusalem **JORDAN** An Najaf An Nasiriya Esfahan Yazd **IRAN** Chardzhou Bukhara
Tanta Port Said Ma'an Basra Ahvaz Khorramshahr 4548 Tabas Gonabad Herat Bairam-Ali
Cairo Suez Abadan Abadan 4075 Birjand Maimana **AFGHANISTAN** Farah
El Faiyum Ismailia **KUWAIT** Bandar Khomeyni Shiraz Anar Mazar-e Sharif Girishk Qandahar

C

Sinai 2637 Kuwait Khoemeyni Kazerun Kerman Helmand **PAKIS**
Al Jawf Hail Turabah Shatt al Arab Jahrom Zahedan Quetta Nushki
Ras Banas Al'Ula Buraydah Bushehr Bandar Abbas Dasht Central Makran Ra. Shikarpur
Yenbo N Buraydah The Gulf Jask Bam Gulf of Oman Gwadar Nawabshah
Quseir W. Hamd Medina **SAUDI** Al Qatif Dammam Str. of Hormuz Pasni
Rabigh Mubarraz **BAHRAIN** Sharjah Dubai Ormara Karachi
Halaib Jedda **ARABIA** Riyadh Al-Hufuf **QATAR** Doha Abu Dhabi As Sohar 3048 **Muscat** Indus Delta
Mecca Taif **UNITED ARAB EMIRATES** Ras al Hadd Tropic of Cancer
Port Sudan Sulaiyil Layla Ras al Madraka

D

Suakin 'Asir Abha Rub' al Khali **OMAN** G. of Masirah
Massawa Farasan Is. (Empty Quarter) Kuria Muria Is.
ERITREA Asmera Dahlak Arch. Amran Shibam Mirbat
Al Hudaydah Sana' Hadhramaut Ras Fartak
Dese **ETHIOPIA** Ta'izz Yarim **YEMEN** Sayhut Ras al Hadd
Mussa Ali 2066 Bab el Mandeb Shuqra Mukalla
DJIBOUTI Aden Madinat al Shaab **Gulf of Aden** Socotra (Yemen)
Djibouti Berbera

E

Dire Dawa Harer Erigavo Ras Asir (C. Guardafui)
Hargeisa Hordio **ARABIAN**
Ogaden Bender Beila **SEA**
Gabredarre
SOMALI REP. Ilig Obbia
Shibeli **I N D I A**
Mogadishu

Projection : Alber's Equal Area with two standard parallels

East from Greenwich

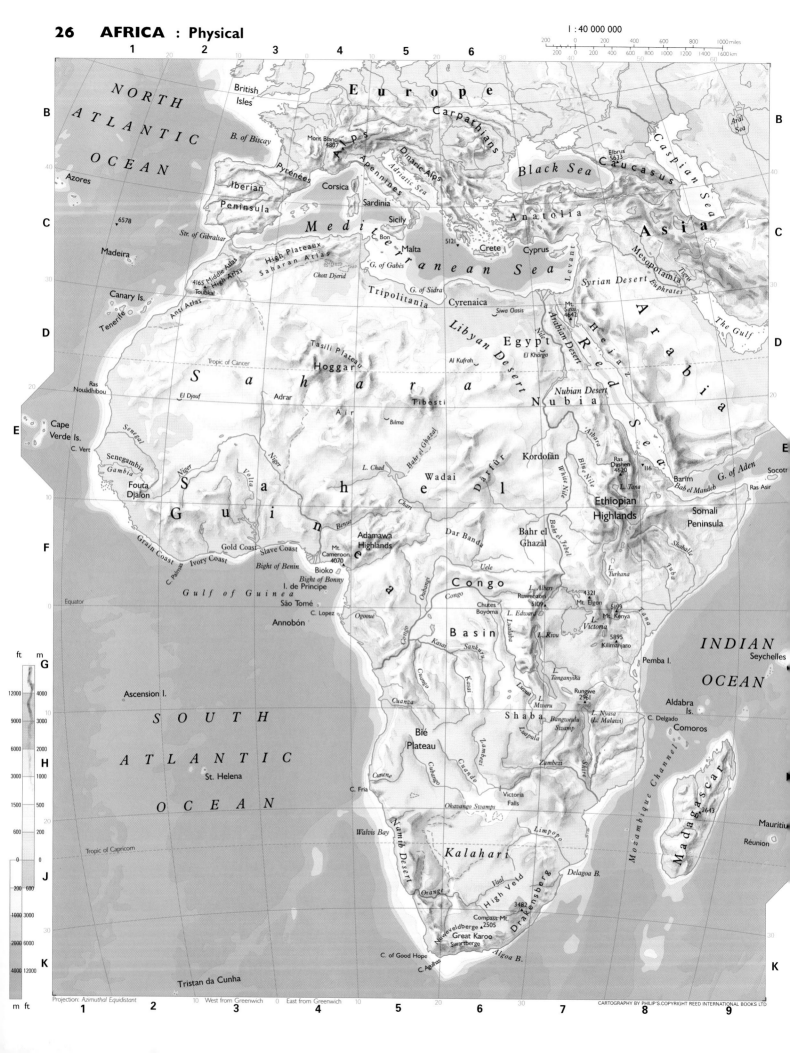

1 : 40 000 000

1 : 40 000 000

200   0   200   400   600   800   1000 miles
200   0   200   400   600   800   1000   1200   1400   1600 km

4   5   6   7   8   9   10

NORTH ATLANTIC OCEAN

UNITED KINGDOM
LONDON
NETH.
BELG.
PARIS
FRANCE
GERMANY
POLAND   Warsaw
Prague
CZECH REP.
Vienna   SLOVAK REP.
SWITZ.   AUSTRIA   HUNGARY
CROATIA   ROMANIA
BOS.-HERZ.   YUG.
ITALY   MAC.
Rome   BULGARIA
Sardinia   ALB.
Corsica
Adriatic Sea
GREECE   Athens
Crete   CYPRUS
MALTA
Sicily

RUSSIA
Kiev
UKRAINE   Volgograd
KAZAKSTAN
Odessa
Black Sea   Aral Sea
GEORGIA
ARM.   AZER.   Baku
Ankara   Caspian Sea   TURKMEN.
TURKEY
Aleppo   Mosul
SYRIA   Tigris   Esfahān
LEB.   Damascus   Baghdad
Tel Aviv   Euphrates   IRAQ   IRAN
Jaffa   Jerusalem   Syrian Desert
ISRAEL   JORDAN   Basra
Port Said   Suez   KUWAIT
Alexandria   CAIRO   The Gulf

B. of Biscay

Azores (Port.)

Madrid
PORTUGAL   SPAIN
Lisbon

Madeira (Port.)

Canary Is. (Sp.)

Algiers   Annaba
Constantine   Tunis
TUNISIA   Tripoli
Rabat   Tétouan   Sfax
Casablanca   Fès
MOROCCO   Chott Djerid
Marrakesh
Mediterranean Sea
Misrātah   Benghazi

Ras Nouâdhibou
El Aaiún
WESTERN SAHARA
Dakhla
Fdérik

A L G E R I A   In Salah   **L I B Y A**
Marzūq
Al Jawf
Tropic of Cancer

S a h a r a

EGYPT   Red Sea
El Faiyûm
Asyût   Nile
Aswân
Wadi Halfa   Medina
Port Sudan   Jedda   Mecca
SAUDI ARABIA   BAHRAIN   QATAR
Riyadh

MAURITANIA
Nouakchott
Tombouctou
Senegal
St-Louis
C. Vert   Agades
Dakar   **N I G E R**   **C H A D**
SENEGAL   Niamey
GAMBIA   Banjul   MALI   BURKINA   Kano
GUINEA-BISSAU   Bissau   FASO   Ndjamena
Bamako   Ouagadougou   Maiduguri
GUINEA   Bobo-Dioulasso
Conakry   BENIN   **N I G E R I A**
Freetown   IVORY   GHANA   Abuja
SIERRA LEONE   COAST   TOGO   Ibadan
Yamoussoukro   Kumasi   Lomé   Lagos   Enugu
Monrovia   LIBERIA   Bouaké   Porto Novo
Abidjan   Accra   **CAMEROON**
Sekondi-Takoradi   Douala   Yaoundé

Atbara   Atbara   Mesewa
Omdurmân   Khartoum   ERITREA   Asmera
S U D A N   Wâd Medani   YEMEN
El Fâsher   White Nile   Blue Nile   DJIBOUTI   G. of Aden
El Obeid   L. Tana   Djibouti   Socotra (Yemen)
Chari   Malakâl   Addis Ababa   Berbera   Ras Asir
Abéché   Bahr el Jebel   Wau   ETHIOPIA   Harer
L. Chad   **CENTRAL   AFRICAN REP.**   Benue
Bangui   SOMALI REP.
Shabelle

Bight of Benin
Port Harcourt
Malabo
EQUATORIAL GUINEA
SÃO TOMÉ & PRINCIPE
Libreville
Annobón
C. Lopez

Gulf of Guinea

Equator

Ubangi   L. Turkana
Congo   Kisangani   KENYA   Juba
Mbandaka   L. Albert   UGANDA   Kismayu
GABON   CONGO   Kampala   Kisumu   Nairobi
(DEM. REP. OF THE)   L. Edward   L. Victoria
Brazzaville   Kasai   RWANDA   Kigali   Mombasa
Pointe Noire   Kinshasa   BURUNDI   Bujumbura
CABINDA   Matadi   TANZANIA   Zanzibar
(Angola)   Kananga   Dodoma   Dar es Salaam
L. Tanganyika
Mogadishu

INDIAN OCEAN

SEYCHELLES

SOUTH ATLANTIC OCEAN

Ascension I. (U.K.)

Luanda   Likasi   L. Mweru   C. Delgado   COMOROS
Lobito   Lubumbashi   L. Malawi   Antsiranana
A N G O L A   Ndola   Mayotte (Fr.)
Huambo   ZAMBIA   MALAWI   Mahajanga
Namibe   Lusaka   Lilongwe   Moçambique
Cuando   Zambezi   Blantyre   Toamasina
Cunene   Livingstone   Harare   MOZAMBIQUE   MADAGASCAR   MAURITIUS
St. Helena (U.K.)   Bulawayo   Beira   Antananarivo
NAMIBIA   ZIMBABWE   Fianarantsoa   Réunion (Fr.)
Limpopo   Mozambique Channel
BOTSWANA   Aldabra Is.
Windhoek   Gaborone
Tropic of Capricorn
Johannesburg   Pretoria   Maputo
Kimberley   Mbabane   SWAZ.
Orange   Vaal   Maseru   LESOTHO
SOUTH AFRICA   Durban
Cape Town   East London
C. of Good Hope   Port Elizabeth
C. Agulhas

Tristan da Cunha (U.K.)

Projection: Azimuthal Equidistant

West from Greenwich   East from Greenwich

● Dakar   Capital Cities

CARTOGRAPHY BY PHILIP'S

1   2   3   4   5   6   7   8   9

NORTH ATLANTIC

OCEAN

6578

SPAIN

Málaga · Almería
Cádiz
Gibraltar (U.K.) · Str. of Gibraltar
Tangier · Ceuta (Sp.) · Tétouan · Al Hoceima · Melilla (Sp.)
Larache · Ksar el Kebir · Ouezzane · Sidi-Bel-Abbès · Oran
Kenitra · Salé · Fès · Toza · Tlemcen · Saïda
Rabat · Meknès · Jerada
Casablanca
El Jadida · Berrechid · Khenifra · Bouârfa
Settat · Khouribga · Beni Mellal
Safi · **MOROCCO** · Ar Rachidya · Figuig · Beni Ounif
Essaouira · Dj. Toubkal 4165 · Ouarzazate · Abadla · Béchar
Marrakesh · Anti Atlas
C. Rhir · Agadir · Taroudannt · Igli · Beni Abbès
Ifni · Tiznit · Dra · Mengoub · Kerzaz

Algiers · Harrach · Tizi-Ouzou · Bejaïa · Skikda · Annaba
Mostaganem · Ech Cheliff · Blida · Médéa · Constantine · Sétif · Guelma
Mascara · Ksar el Boukhari · Batna · Khenchela · Aïn Beïda
El Aricha · Tiaret · Bou Saâda · Biskra
Mecheria 2235 · El Bayadh · Djelfa · Touggourt · El Oued · Gafsa
Ghardaïa · Laghouat · Ouargla · Hassi Messaoud · Ghudâmis

Madeira (Port.) · Pto. Santo · Funchal

Canary Is. (Sp.)
La Palma · Lanzarote · Arrecife
Tenerife · Fuerteventura · Puerto del Rosario
Gomera 3718 · Sta. Cruz · Gran Canaria · Las Palmas
Hierro · C. Juby · Tarfaya

ALGERIA
Bou Izakarn · Tindouf · Adrar · In Belbel · In Salah · Ohanem
El Aaiún · Semara · Bj. Fly Ste. Marie · Zaouiet Reggane · Aoulef el Arab · Bordj Omar Driss
Bu Craa · Aïn Ben Tili · Chegga · Timimoun · Miliana · Illizi
Dakhla · Bir Mogrein · Terhazza · Ouallene
C. Barbas · Fdérik · Zouérate · Taoudenni · Arak · Bj.-in-Eker · Idelès · Djanet
WESTERN SAHARA · Erg · Chech · Tanezrouft · Hoggar · Tahat 2918 · Tamanrasset
Nouâdhibou · Châr · Poste Maurice Cortier · Adrar des Iforhas · Admer
Ras Nouâdhibou / La Güera · Atâr · Ouadâne · Mabrouk · Aïr · Monts Tamgak
Chinguetti · Araouane · Kidal · Iférouâne · 1900 · Aoudéras
C. Timiris · Oujeft · Tichit · Bou Djébéha · In-Gall · Agadez
Nouakchott · Rachid · Tidjikja · Akreijit · **NIGER**
Boutilimit · Moudjéria · Togba · Tombouctou · Bamba · Kerchoual
Mederdra · Aleg · Tâmchekket · Oualâta · Goundam · Diré · Gourma-Rharous · Gao · Ménaka · Tahoua · Tanout
St. Louis · Pador · Bogué · Kiffa · Néma · Niafouke · Ansongo · Hombori · Tamaské · Gangara · Kellé
Rosso · Dagana · Kaédi · Mbout · **MAURITANIA** · Bâssikounou · Nioro du Sahel · Nara · Madaoua · Birni Nkonni · Zinder · Baultoum
Louga · Matam · Linguére · Sélibaby · Yélimané · Douentza · Filingué · Marâdi · Nguru
Tivaouane · Dahra · Bakel · Kayes · Mourdiah · Sokolo · Sagala · Mopti · Djibo · Dori · Téra · Tillabéri · Sokoto · Gusau · Katsina · Hadejia
Thies · Diourbel · Kayes · Didiéni · Ké-Macina · Bandiagara · Famalé · Niamey · Dosso · Gandi · Kaura · Azare
Dakar · Kaolack · Kaffrine · Bafoulabé · **MALI** · Sarra · Ségou · Djenné · Toupan · Ouahigouya · Kaya · Say · Argungu · Birnin Kebbi · Jega · Gummi · Dangora · Potiskum
Mbour · **SENEGAL** · Tambacounda · Satadougou · Kita · Banamba · Niger · San · Bobo-Dioulasso · **BURKINA FASO** · Yako · N'Gourma · Diapaga · Goya · Kende · Shanga · Kaduna · Zaria
GAMBIA · Georgetown · Kolda · Kédougou · Koulikoro · Douna · Koutiala · Douentza · Ouagadougou · Boromo · Léo · Pama · Kandi · Babana · Kainji · Bida · **NIGERIA** · Kafanchan
Banjul · Ziguinchor · Farim · **GUINEA-BISSAU** · Bafatá · Bamako · Sikasso · Banfora · Diébougou · Léo · Mango · Nikki · Jebba · Ningi · Bauchi
Bissau · Balama · Gaoual · Fouta Djalon · Dinguiraye · Siguiri · Tingrela · Sidéradougou · Gaoua · Wa · Savelugu · Jougou · Kaiama · Parakou · Ilorin · Oyo · Ife · Lokoja · Makurdi · Wukari
Victoria · Boké · Labé · Tougué · Kankan · Bougouni · Tiébissou · Boundiali · Bouna · Gambaga · Tamale · Salaga · Shaki · Ogbomosho · Oshogbo · Benin City · Enugu
Conakry · Forécariah · Kabala 1948 · Kissidougou · Odienné · Kornogo · Kong · Dâboya · Sokodé · Igbetti · Iwo · Ibadan · Ado-Ekiti · Owo · Onitsha · Calabar
SIERRA LEONE · Magburaka · Guékédou · Beyla · Koro · **IVORY COAST** · Katiola · Bondoukou · Kintampo · Yeji · **TOGO** · Atakpamé · Abeokuta · Benin City · Aba · **CAMEROON**
Freetown · Waterloo · Pendembu · Macenta · Touba · Mankono · Dabakala · Berekum · Wenchi · **GHANA** · Lake Volta · Blitta · Kpalimé · Lagos · Ondo · Sapele · Port Harcourt · Mont Cameroun 4070 · Douala
Sherbro I. · Moyamba · Bo · Kenema · Séguéla · Bouaké · Bocanda · **BENIN** · Kumasi · Nkawkaw · Koforidua · Porto-Novo · Cotonou · Warri · Okrika · Bioko · Limbe
Bonthe · Sulima · Man · Danane · Daloa · Dimbokro · Obuasi · Oda · Tema · Accra · Bight of Benin · Rey Malabo
LIBERIA · Guiglo · Yamoussoukro · Dunkwa · Aného · Winneba · Cape Coast
Monrovia · Careysburg · Tapeta · Agboville · Prestea · Sekondi-Takoradi
Marshall · Buchanan · Toulepleu · Lakota · Abidjan · Grand Bassam · Axim
River Cess · Greenville · Tabou · Sassandra · Grand Lahou · C. Three Points
Garawe · C. Palmas · San Pédro · Tai · Graba

Projection: Sanson Flamsteed's Sinusoidal

West from Greenwich · East from Greenwich

1 : 20 000 000

100 0 100 200 300 400 miles

100 0 100 200 300 400 500 600 km

MEDITERRANEAN SEA

TURKEY

Antalya Iskenderun Aleppo Mosul

Rhodes Antakya Latakia **SYRIA** Mesopotamia

CYPRUS Nicosia Hama Euphrates

Crete Iraklion Limassol Tripoli Homs **IRAQ**

LEBANON Ar Rutbah

Beirut Damascus

'Akko Haifa Amman **JORDAN**

ISRAEL Jerusalem

Tel Aviv-Jaffa Be'er Sheva

Gaza Khan Yunis Dead Sea

El 'Arīsh Ma'ān

Port Said El Qantara Elat Al 'Aqabah Al Jawf

Damietta Ismaïlia

Alexandria Mahalla el Kubra Suez Tabūk **SAUDI**

Damanhūr Mansūra Nafud Desert

Rashīd Tanta Zagazig Sinai Pen.

Al Jaghbūb Qāra **CAIRO** Helwân Al Muwaylih Madā'in Salih

El Giza Sinnūris Taymā'

Qattâra Depression **El Faiyum** Beni Suef Al Wajh **ARABIA**

Sīwa Beni Mazār Arabian

El Bawiti **El Minya** Mallawi Desert Umm Lajj

Asyūt Manfalūt Abu Tig Dairūt Būr Safâga Medina

Qasr Farâfra Sohâg Tahta Akhmîm Quseir

L I B Y A N **D E S E R T** Girga Qena

El Qasr El Khârga Luxor Qûs Yanbu'al Bahr

El Wâhât el-Dakhla Mût Isna

El Wâhât el-Khârga Bârîs Idfu Rabigh Qasr

1st Cataract **Aswân** Jedda At Ta'if

Aswân High Dam El Shallal Mecca Al Lith

Dunqul Bîr Shalatein Lake Nasser Bîr Ungât Halaiba

E G Y P T

L I B Y A

Tropic of Cancer

Kufra Oasis

J. Uweinat 1893 El Wâhât el Selîma Wadi Halfa Gebeit Mine **RED SEA**

Ayn al 'Uwaynat Kosha Abri **N u b i a n   D e s e r t** Muhammad Qol

Laqiya Arba'in Delgo Muhammad Qol

C H A D Nukheila 3rd Cataract Dongola Abu Hamed Port Sudan

Bir 'Atrun Argo El Kab Abū Dis Suakin

El Khandaq Kareima 4th Cataract 5th Cataract Sinkat Trinkitat

Ed Debba Merowe Berber Haiya Junction Tokar 'Aqig

Korti Atbara Musmar Derudeb

Ed Dâmer Adarama Karora

Wad Hamid Shendi

6th Cataract Geili Nakfa **ERITREA**

Omdurmân El Khartûm Bahrî Keren Mitsiwa

Khartoum El Kamlin Kassala Akordat Asmera Zula

Malha **S U D A N** Khashm El Girba Barentu Adwa

Tiné El Wuz El Geteina Rufa'a **Wâd Medanî** el Girba Adwa

Shigaiba Hamrat esh Sheykh Gedaref Aksum

Arada Biltine Kutum Sodirî Kagmar Ed Dueim Singa Gallabât Metema 4620 Mekele

Kabkabiyah El Fâsher Umm Keddada Ed Dueim Sennâr Ras Dashen Sekota

Al Junaynah Zalingei Wad Banda Umm Bel Baro El Mafâza L. Tana Lalibela

J. Marrah 3088 Nyâlâ En Nahud Abū Zabad Umm Ruwaba Er Roseires Gonder Debre Tabor

D a r f u r Taweisha El Odaiya Dilling Rashad Renk Blue Nile Gamaka Mekdela

Idd al Ghanam Rahad al Bardî Buram Muglad El Laqâwa Heiban Kurmuk Mota

Kafia Kingi Nyâmlêll Kâdugli Talodi Kako Melut Nekemte Debre Markos

Abyssinia Tungaru Kodok Gimbi **Addis Ababa**

Songo Birao Buram Bahr el 'Arab Benti Malakâl Addis Alem

Quanda Djallé **K o r d o f a n** Gogrial White Nile Abwong Dembidolo

Dem Zubeir **J u r S u d d** Meshra er Req Fangak Nasir Gore **ETHIOPIA**

Wâw Bahr el Jebel Duk Faiwal Sobat Gambela L. Ziway

CENTRAL AFRICAN REPUBLIC Rumbêk Kongor Jima L. Shala

Tonj Pibor P. Mâji L. Abaya 4200 Chencha

Yirol Bôr L. Shamo

Tali P. Tombe Gidole Burji

Tamburâ Amadi Kapoeta Chew Bahir Arero

Maridî Jûba Mega

Yambio Yei Kâjo Kaji Lokitaung Todenyang

Torit **KENYA** L. Turkana

1 : 8 000 000

50   0   50   100   150   200 miles
50   0   100   200   300 km

COPYRIGHT GEORGE PHILIP LTD

CHAD

Lake Chad

NIGER

MALI

BURKINA FASO

Ouagadougou

Niamey

BENIN

TOGO

Cotonou
Lomé
Porto-Novo
Ouidah

ACCRA
Tema
Winneba
Cape Coast
Sekondi-Takoradi

GHANA

NORTHERN

ASHANTI

BRONG-AHAFO

EASTERN
CENTRAL

Kumasi
Nkawkaw
Kade
Nsawam

Bolgatanga
Tamale
Yendi

IVORY COAST

Lake Volta

NIGERIA

SOKOTO
KATSINA
KANO
JIGAWA
YOBE
BORNO
KADUNA
KEBBI
NIGER
KWARA
OYO
OGUN
LAGOS
ONDO
EDO
DELTA
EDO
ANAMBRA
ENUGU
IMO
ABIA
CROSS RIVER
RIVER
BAUCHI
PLATEAU
TARABA
ADAMAWA
BENUE
KOGI
FED. CAP. TERR.

Abuja

LAGOS
IBADAN
Abeokuta
Ife
Ilesha
Oshogbo
Ede
Iwo
Ogbomosho
Oyo
Ilorin
Offa
Ila
Akure
Ondo
Benin City
Sapele
Warri
Port Harcourt
Calabar
Enugu
Onitsha
Aba
Owerri
Umuahia
Okigwi
Abakaliki

Kano
Kaduna
Zaria
Katsina
Gusau
Sokoto
Birnin Kebbi
Argungu
Kontagora
Minna
Bida
Lokoja
Makurdi
Lafia
Jos
Bauchi
Gombe
Azare
Hadejia
Nguru
Gashua
Potiskum
Damaturu
Maiduguri
Dikwa
Biu
Numan
Yola
Jalingo
Wukari
Shendam

Yaoundé
DOUALA
Buea
Kumba
Bamenda
Tiko

CAMEROUN

EQUATORIAL GUINEA

BIOKO
Rey Malaba

GULF OF GUINEA

Bight of Benin

Niger Delta

East from Greenwich

Projection Lambert's Equivalent Azimuthal

1 : 8 000 000

50   0   50   100   150   200 miles
50   0   100   200   300 km

MOZAMBIQUE

ZIMBABWE

Bulawayo

Maputo

SWAZILAND

BOTSWANA

NAMIBIA

Namib Desert

Kalahari

Windhoek

Tropic of Capricorn

NORTHERN PROVINCE

MPUMALANGA

PRETORIA
JOHANNESBURG
Germiston
Soweto
Krugersdorp
Vereeniging

KWAZULU

NATAL

PIETERMARITZBURG
DURBAN
Umlazi
KwaMashu

FREE STATE

Bloemfontein

LESOTHO
Maseru

Kroonstad
Welkom
Virginia

NORTH WEST

Kimberley

SOUTH AFRICA

NORTHERN CAPE

EASTERN CAPE

Queenstown
Umtata
East London
King William's Town
Bisho
Grahamstown
PORT ELIZABETH
Uitenhage

De Aar
Middelburg
Graaff-Reinet
Cradock
Beaufort West

WESTERN CAPE

Oudtshoorn
George
Mosselbaai
Swellendam
Worcester
Paarl
Stellenbosch
CAPE TOWN
Table Mt 1086
C. of Good Hope
C. Agulhas

INDIAN OCEAN

ATLANTIC OCEAN

Walvis Bay

COPYRIGHT GEORGE PHILIP & SON Ltd

Projection: Lambert's Equivalent Azimuthal

East from Greenwich

ETHIOPIA

KENYA

SUDAN

CHAD

NIGER

NIGERIA

CAMEROON

CENTRAL AFRICAN REPUBLIC

GABON

CONGO

CONGO (DEM. REP. OF THE)

TANZANIA

RWANDA

BURUNDI

CABINDA

EQUATORIAL GUINEA

ERITREA

Addis Ababa · Khartoum · Omdurman · Nairobi · Kampala · Kigali · Bujumbura · Dodoma · Dar-es-Salaam · Kinshasa · Brazzaville · Bangui · Ndjamena · Yaoundé · Douala · Libreville · Luanda · Kananga · Kisangani · Bukavu · Zanzibar · Mombasa · Kassala · Asmera · Mekele · Gonder · L. Tana · L. Victoria · L. Tanganyika · L. Turkana (L. Rudolf) · L. Chad · L. Albert · L. Kivu · L. Edward · L. Mweru

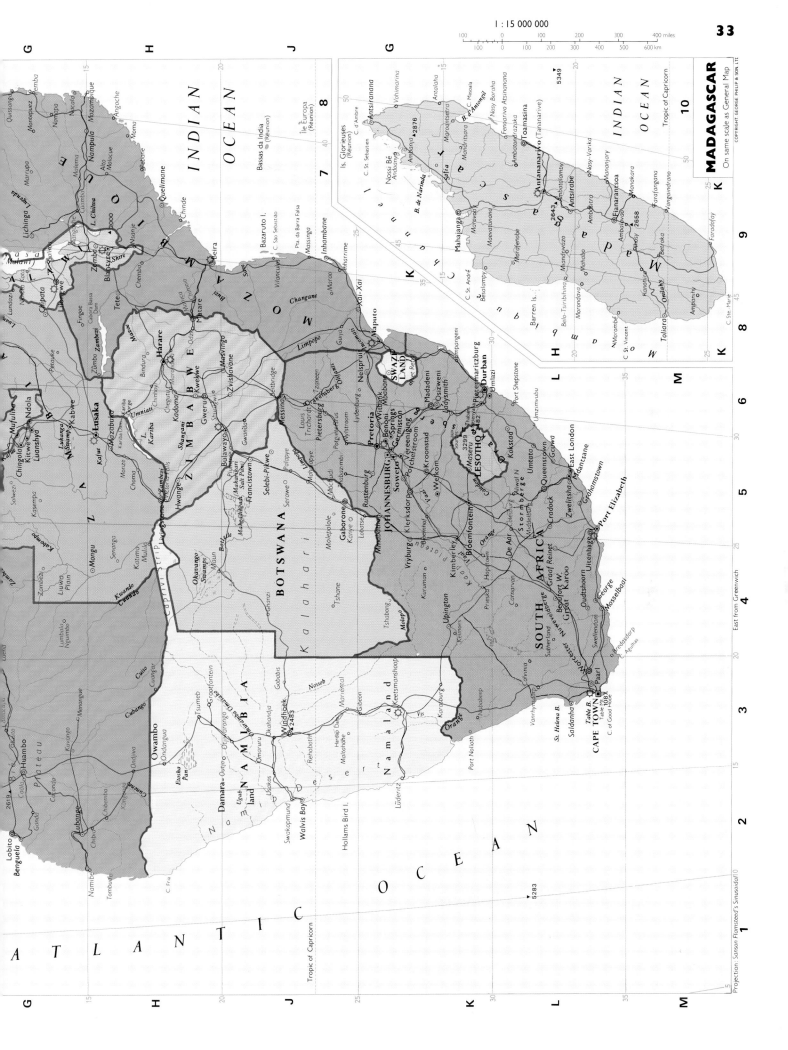

1 : 15 000 000

100   0   100   200   300   400 miles
100   0   100   200   300   400   500   600 km

MADAGASCAR
On same scale as General Map

COPYRIGHT GEORGE PHILIP & SON, LTD.

INDIAN   OCEAN

Tropic of Capricorn

Antsiranana
Vohémarina
Antalaha
C. d'Ambre   C. Masoala
B. d'Antongil
5349
2876   Nosy Boraha
Ambanja   Maroantsetra
Mandritsara   Fenoarivo Atsinanana
Sofia   Mananara
Ambatondrazaka   Toamasina (Tamatave)
Antananarivo (Tananarive)
Moramanga
Ambatolampy
2643   Antsirabe
Morondava   Mandoto   Ambositra
Ambalavao   Fianarantsoa
2658   Ihosy   Ambohimahasoa
Farafangana
Vangaindrano

Mahajanga
Muevatanana
Besalampy

Barren Is.

Belo-Tsiribihina
Morondava
Mahabo
Manja

C. St. André

Morombé   Ankazoabo
C. St. Vincent
Toliara

Ampanihy
Betroka
Kanotina   Onilahy   Ambovombe
C. Ste. Marie   Faradofay

INDIAN   OCEAN

 Is. Glorieuses
(Réunion)

Nossi Bé
Andoany
C. St. Sebastien

B. de Narinda

INDIAN   OCEAN

Quissanga
Montepuez   Pemba
Nampula   Nacala
Marrupa   Alto
Molocue   Angoche
Lichinga   Nampula   Mozambique
Lugenda   L. Chilwa
3000   Moma
Cuamba
Mozambique   Pebane

Zomba   Shire
Blantyre   Quelimane
Chinde
Tete   Chemba
Cabora Bassa Dam
Chimoio   Nsanje   Bazaruto I.
Vilanculos   C. São Sebastião
Mutare   Pta. da Barra Falsa
Inhambane
Massinga
Save   Vilanculos   Maxixe

INDIAN

OCEAN

ile Europa
(Réunion)

Bassas da India
(Réunion)

MOZAMBIQUE

Beira

Quissico
Xai-Xai
Inharrime
Changane

Limpopo

Maputo

SWAZI
LAND

Nelspruit   Komatipoort
Mbabane
Wet Reef
Osizweni   Madadeni
Ladysmith   Pietermaritzburg
Pretoria   Pinetown   Durban
Witbank   Umlazi
Benoni   Springs
Germiston   Port Shepstone
JOHANNESBURG   Umzimvubu
Soweto   Vereeniging
Klerksdorp   Vryheid
Kroonstad   Welkom
Umtata

2482   3299   LESOTHO
Maseru   Kokstad

Mdantsane
Queenstown
East London
King William's Town
Stormberge
Cradock   Grahamstown
Port Elizabeth
Uitenhage

Kimberley
Bloemfontein
Kuruman
Upington   Hopetown
De Aar
Orange   Colesberg
Graaff Reinet
Beaufort W.
Great Karoo   George
Oudtshoorn   Mossel Bay

SOUTH   AFRICA

Springbok
Carnarvon
Sutherland
Calvinia
Worcester   Swellendam
Paarl   Bredasdorp
CAPE TOWN   C. Agulhas
Table B.   1087
Table Mt.
C. of Good Hope   St. Helena B.
Saldanha
Port Nolloth

ZAMBIA
Lusaka   Kabwe
Kitwe   Ndola
Chingola   Mufulira
Kabwe   Mazabuka
Kafue   L. Kariba
Monze   Choma
Mongu   Senanga   Livingstone
Sesheke   Kazungula
Victoria Falls
Hwange   Kariba
Katima   Mulilo
Luwa   Plain

ZIMBABWE
Harare
Kadoma   Marondera
Chinhoyi   Bindura
Kwekwe   Masvingo
Gweru   Zvishavane
Bulawayo   Chiredzi
Gwanda   Beitbridge
Plumtree   Messina

BOTSWANA
Kasane
Maun   Nata
Okavango   Serowe
Swamps   Mahalapye   Selebi-Pikwe
Ghanzi   Palapye
Kang   Mochudi   Francistown
Tshane   Gaborone   Lobatse
Molepolole   Kanye
Tshabong   Mafikeng
Rustenburg

Kalahari

NAMIBIA
Windhoek   2483
Tsumeb
Grootfontein
Okahandja
Gobabis
Omaruru
Rehoboth
Mariental
Keetmanshoop
Lüderitz
Karasburg

Owambo
Etosha Pan
Ondangua
Ondangua

Walvis Bay
Swakopmund
Hollams Bird I.

Namaland

Namib   Desert

ANGOLA
Lobito
Benguela
Huambo
Lubango
Namibe
Tombua
C. Frio

ATLANTIC   OCEAN

Tropic of Capricorn

5283

East from Greenwich

Projection: Sanson Flamsteed's Sinusoidal

G   H   J   K   L   M

G   H   J   K   L   M

INDONESIA

Sulawesi (Celebes)
Kendari
5300
Butung
Ujung Pandang (Makasar)

Buru
Ambon
Ceram
Misool
Sorong
Vogelkop
Fakfak
Irian Jaya
Pegunungan Maoke
Puncak Jaya
5020
Jayapura
Biak

PAPUA NEW GUINEA
Wewak
Madang
Mount Hagen
4508 Mt. Wilhelm
Lae
New Guinea
Fly
Owen Stanley Range
Gulf of Papua
Port Moresby
D'Entrecasteau
Louisiade Archipelago

Bismarck Archipelago
Kavieng
New Ireland
Rabaul
New Britain
9140
Solomon Sea

Kai Is.
7260
3350
Aru Is.
Banda Sea

Wetar
Babar
Leti
Tanimbar Is.
Pulau Yos Sudarso

Flores Sea
Alor
Dili EAST TIMOR 3310
Timor
Timor Sea
Arafura Sea
Torres Strait
C. York

Sumbawa
Rube
Flores
Ende
Kupang
Sumba
6204

Melville I.
C. Croker
Darwin
Arnhem Land
C. Arnhem
Gulf of Carpenteria
Wellesley I.
Weipa
Cape York Peninsula
Great Barrier Reef
Coral
Sea
Coral Sea Islands
Territory

C. Londonderry
Wyndham
Kimberley Plateau
Derby
Broome
Cambridge G.

Daly Waters
Larrimah
Tennant Creek
NORTHERN
Tanami Desert
Barkly Tableland
Mount Isa
Normanton
Forsayth
Kajaabi
Flinders
Mitchell
Cooktown
Cairns
1611 Bartle Frere
Townsville
Charters Towers
Hughenden
Mackay

TERRITORY

AUSTRALIA

Great Sandy Desert
L. Mackay
Gibson Desert
Lake Disappointment
Macdonnell Ranges
1510 Mt. Ziel
Alice Springs
Simpson Desert
Winton
Longreach
Yaraka
QUEENSLAND
Rockhampton
Gladstone
Bundaberg
Maryborough
Gympie
Roma
Great Dividing Range
Diamantina

Port Hedland
Dampier
N.W. Cape
Mt. Bruce 1226
Hamersley Range
Newman
Carnarvon
Meekatharra
WESTERN
Leonora
L. Carnegie
Great Victoria Desert
AUSTRALIA
Geraldton
Lake Barlee
Kalgoorlie-Boulder
Norseman
Murchison
Northam
Perth
Bunbury
C. Leeuwin
Augusta
Albany
Esperance

Ayers Rock
Mt. Woodroffe 1440
Musgrave Ranges
SOUTH
AUSTRALIA
Cooper Creek
Lake Eyre
Marree
Tarcoola
Penong
Deakin
Nullarbor Plain
Great Australian Bight
5632

Grey Range
Charleville
Quilpie
Cunnamulla
Thargomindah
Bourke
Warrego
Darling
Cobar
Dirranbandi
Walgett
Dubbo
Orange
NEW SOUTH
WALES
Newcastle
Bathurst
SYDNEY
Wollongong
Shellharbour
Canberra
CAPITAL TERRITORY
Tamworth
1615 Round Mt.
Taree
Lismore
Gold Coast
Ipswich
BRISBANE
Toowoomba

Flinders Range
Broken Hill
Port Augusta
Port Pirie
Whyalla
Spencer Gulf
Port Lincoln
Kangaroo I.
Adelaide
Murray
Mildura
Encounter B.
Wagga Wagga
Albury
Shepparton
Murray
Mt. Kosciusko 2237
Australian Alps
Bombala
C. Howe
VICTORIA
Horsham
Bendigo
Ballarat
MELBOURNE
Geelong
Warrnambool
Mount Gambier

Goulburn
INDIAN OCEAN
King I.
Bass Strait
Furneaux Group

TASMANIA
Burnie
1617 Mt. Ossa
Launceston
Hobart
S.E. Cape

Darling Range

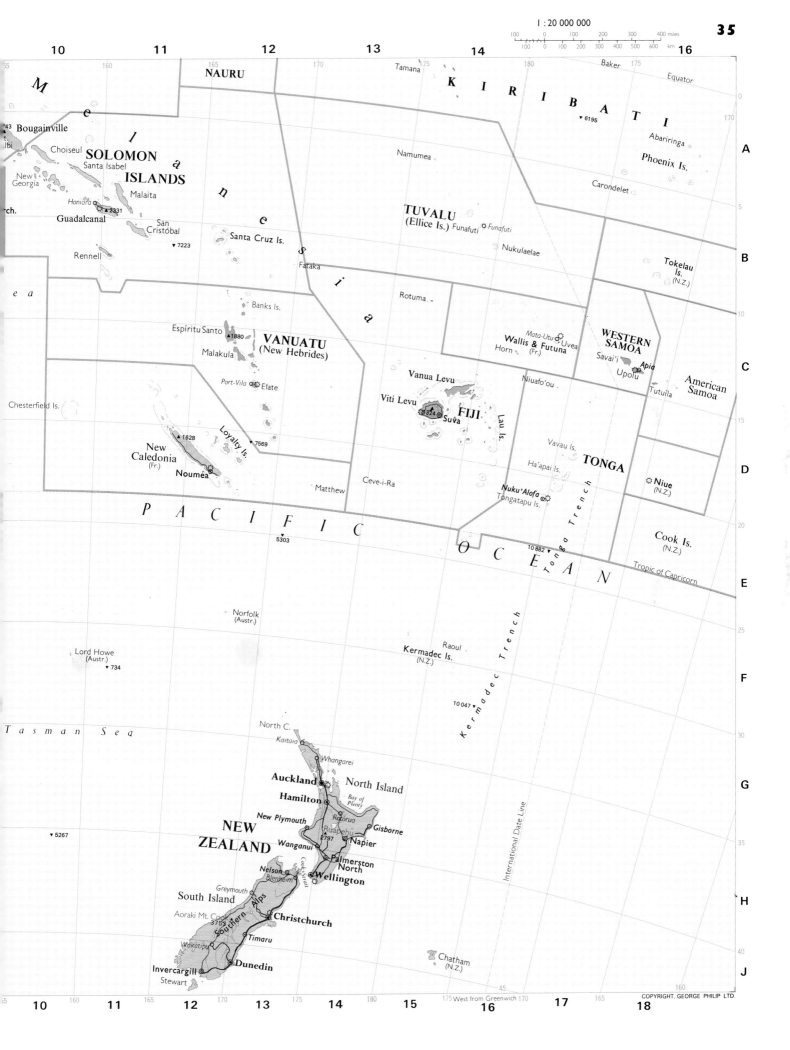

1 : 20 000 000

100   0   100   200   300   400 miles
100 0 100 200 300 400 500 600 km

Tamana   Baker   Equator

K I R I B A T I

Bougainville
Ibi

Choiseul   ▼ 6195
Santa Isabel   Abariringa
SOLOMON
New   **Phoenix Is.**
Georgia
ISLANDS   Namumea

rch.   Carondelet

Honiara ○ ▲ 2331   **TUVALU**
Malaita   (Ellice Is.)   Funafuti ○ Funafuti
Guadalcanal
San   Nukulaelae
Cristóbal   **Tokelau**
Rennell   ▼ 7223   Santa Cruz Is.   **Is.**
                                                                (N.Z.)
e a   Fataka
                                        Rotuma

Banks Is.   Mata-Utu ○
Espíritu Santo ▲ 1880   **Wallis & Futuna**   **WESTERN**
                VANUATU   Horn   Uvea   **SAMOA**
Malakula   (New Hebrides)   (Fr.)   Savai'i ○ Apia
                                              Niuafo'ou   Upolu
Port-Vila ○ Efate   Vanua Levu   Tutuila   **American
Chesterfield Is.   Viti Levu   Samoa**
                                              ▲3524   **FIJI**
                        ▲ 1628   Loyalty Is.   Suva   Vavau Is.
New   ▼ 7569   Lau Is.   **TONGA**
Caledonia   Ha'apai Is.   ○ **Niue**
(Fr.)   Nouméa ○   (N.Z.)
                    Matthew   Ceve-i-Ra   Nuku'Alofa ○
                                                  Tongatapu Is.

P   **A**   **C**   **I**   **F**   **I**   **C**   **Cook Is.**
                                                                                    (N.Z.)
        ▼ 5303   ▼ 10 882   Tropic of Capricorn
                                              O   C   E   A   N

Norfolk
(Austr.)   Raoul
                                              Kermadec Is.
Lord Howe   (N.Z.)
(Austr.)
▼ 734

10 047 ▼

T a s m a n   S e a   North C.
                        Kaitaia ○
                                    Whangarei
                Auckland ○   **North Island**
                Hamilton ○   Bay of
                                  Plenty
                New Plymouth ○   Rotorua
        NEW   Gisborne
        ZEALAND   Wanganui ○ Ruapehu
                                  2797   Napier
▼ 5267   Palmerston
                Nelson ○   North
                Blenheim   ○ **Wellington**
        Greymouth ○ Cook Strait
        South Island   Alps
        Aoraki Mt. Cook   ○ **Christchurch**
              3753   Southern
              Wakatipu ○ Timaru   ○ Chatham
        Invercargill ○ **Dunedin**   (N.Z.)
                Stewart

International Date Line

Kermadec Trench

Tonga Trench

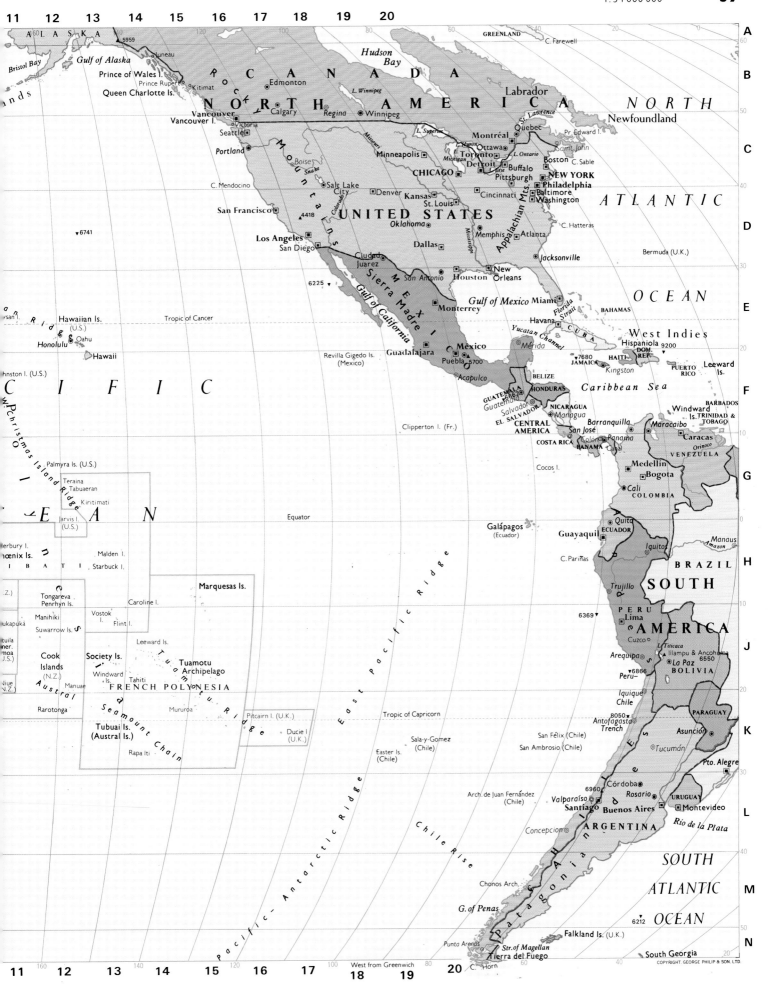

A B C D E F G H J K L M N

11 12 13 14 15 16 17 18 19 20

A L A S K A
5959
Bristol Bay
Gulf of Alaska
Prince of Wales I.
Prince Rupert
Queen Charlotte Is.
Kitimat
Juneau
Edmonton
Vancouver
Vancouver I.
Victoria
Seattle
Calgary
Regina
Winnipeg
L. Winnipeg
Portland
Boise
Snake
C. Mendocino
Salt Lake City
San Francisco
4418
Denver
Kansas
St. Louis
UNITED STATES
Los Angeles
San Diego
Ciudad Juárez
6225
San Antonio
Dallas
Oklahoma
Memphis
Atlanta
Houston
New Orleans
Jacksonville
Monterrey
Gulf of Mexico
Miami
Havana
BAHAMAS
CUBA
Florida Strait
Yucatan Channel
Mérida
Mexico
Guadalajara
Puebla
5700
Acapulco
BELIZE
Yucatan
HONDURAS
GUATEMALA
Guatemala
6662
EL SALVADOR
NICARAGUA
Managua
San José
CENTRAL AMERICA
COSTA RICA
PANAMA
Panama Canal
Colón
Caribbean Sea
Barranquilla
Maracaibo
Caracas
BARBADOS
Windward Is.
TRINIDAD & TOBAGO
PUERTO RICO
Leeward Is.
HAITI
DOM. REP.
JAMAICA
Kingston
7680
Hispaniola
9200
West Indies
ATLANTIC
OCEAN
GREENLAND
C. Farewell
NORTH
C. Hatteras
Bermuda (U.K.)

CANADA
NORTH AMERICA
Hudson Bay
Labrador
Newfoundland
Pr. Edward I.
C. Sable
Saint John
Quebec
Montréal
Ottawa
Toronto
L. Ontario
Boston
Buffalo
Pittsburgh
NEW YORK
Philadelphia
Baltimore
Washington
Cincinnati
Detroit
CHICAGO
Minneapolis
L. Superior
Michigan
Huron
Erie
St. Lawrence
Appalachian Mts.
Missouri
Colorado
Mississippi

Rocky Mountains
Sierra Madre
Gulf of California
M E X I C O

Hawaiian Is. (U.S.)
Honolulu
Oahu
Hawaii
Tropic of Cancer
Revilla Gigedo Is. (Mexico)
Clipperton I. (Fr.)
Cocos I.
Galápagos (Ecuador)
Equator
C. Pariñas
MEDELLÍN
Bogotá
Cali
COLOMBIA
VENEZUELA
Orinoco
Quito
ECUADOR
Guayaquil
Iquitos
Manaus
Amazon
BRAZIL
SOUTH
AMERICA
Trujillo
PERU
Lima
Cuzco
6369
PACIFIC
P A C I F I C
OCEAN
O C E A N

Johnston I. (U.S.)
Christmas Island Ridge
Palmyra Is. (U.S.)
Teraina
Tabuaeran
Kiritimati
Jarvis I. (U.S.)
KIRIBATI
Phoenix Is.
Malden I.
Starbuck I.
Vostok I.
Flint I.
Caroline I.
Marquesas Is.
Tongareva
Penrhyn Is.
Manihiki
Suwarrow Is.
Rakahanga
Pukapuka
Cook Islands (N.Z.)
Society Is.
Windward Is.
Leeward Is.
Tahiti
Manuae
FRENCH POLYNESIA
Tuamotu Archipelago
Tuamotu Ridge
Niue (N.Z.)
Austral
Rarotonga
Tubuai Is. (Austral Is.)
Rapa Iti
Mururoa
Pitcairn I. (U.K.)
Ducie I. (U.K.)
Easter Is. (Chile)
Sala-y-Gomez (Chile)
San Félix (Chile)
San Ambrosio (Chile)
Tropic of Capricorn
8050
Antofagasta Trench
Iquique
Chile
Peru-
6866
La Paz
Illampu & Ancohuma
6550
L. Titicaca
Arequipa
BOLIVIA
PARAGUAY
Asunción
Tucumán
URUGUAY
Montevideo
Pto. Alegre
Córdoba
Rosario
6960
Valparaíso
Santiago
Buenos Aires
Río de la Plata
ARGENTINA
Concepción
Arch. de Juan Fernández (Chile)
Andes
Patagonia
SOUTH
ATLANTIC
OCEAN
Chile Rise
Pacific - Antarctic Ridge
East Pacific Ridge
Seamount Chain
Chonos Arch.
G. of Penas
6212
Punta Arenas
Str. of Magellan
Tierra del Fuego
C. Horn
Falkland Is. (U.K.)
South Georgia

6741

6225

West from Greenwich

11 12 13 14 15 16 17 18 19 20

PACIFIC OCEAN

ALASKA

YUKON TERRITORY

NORTHWEST TERRITORIES

BRITISH COLUMBIA

ALBERTA

SASKATCHEWAN

MANITOBA

Prairies

Canada

Anchorage
Valdez
Seward
Cordova
Mt. St. Elias 5489
Wrangell Mts.
Mt. Sanford 4940
Fairbanks
Tanana
Yukon
Old Crow
Tsiigehtchic
Inuvik
Mackenzie
Ft. Good Hope
Norman Wells
Anderson
Franklin Mts.
C. Bathurst
Banks Island
Amundsen Gulf
C. Baring
Prince Albert Pen.
Prince Albert Sd.
Victoria Island
Wollaston Pen.
Dolphin & Union Str.
Melville Island
Viscount Melville Sound
Prince of Wales Island
M'Clintock Channel
Franklin Str.
Somerset Island
Boothia Peninsula
Coronation Gulf
Coppermine
Kent Pen.
Cambridge Bay
Queen Maud Gulf
Adelaide Pen.
King William I.
Chantrey Inlet
Bathurst Inlet
Echo Bay
Gt. Bear Lake
Gt. Bear
Ft. Simpson
Mackenzie
L. de Gras
Yellowknife
Great Slave L.
Fort Reliance
Clinton Golden L.
Dubawnt L.
L. Garry
Back
Baker L.
Chesterfield I.
Baker Lake
Eskimo Pt.
Nueltin L.

Whitehorse
Skagway
Juneau
Sitka
Baranof I.
Chichagof I.
Pt. of Wales
Wrangell
Dixon Entrance
Pr. Rupert
Portland Can.
Queen Charlotte Is.
Queen Charlotte Sd.
Hecate Str.
Vancouver I.
Q. Charlotte Str.

Watson Lake
Dease Lake
Stikine
Cassiar Mountains
Skeena
Babine L.
Stuart L.
Fraser
Williams L.
Lillooet
Thompson
Prince George
Cariboo Mts.
Quesnel
Mt. Waddington 3994
Squamish
Port Alberni
Nanaimo
VANCOUVER
Victoria
Kamloops
Vernon
Kelowna
Penticton
Bellingham
SEATTLE
Tacoma
Spokane
Yakima
Coeur d'Alene
Kalispell

ALASKA HIGHWAY
Rocky Mountains
Churchill Pk. 3200
Ft. Nelson
Fort Nelson
Ft. St. John
Dawson Creek
Grande Prairie
Smoky
Peace R.
Caribou Mts. 1036
Ft. Vermilion
Peace
Slave
Ft. Smith
Uranium City
Lake Athabasca
Wholdaia L.
Kasba L.
Selkirk Mts.
Kicking Horse P. 1625
Banff
Yellowhead P.
Mt. Robson 3954
Edmonton
Leduc
Wetaskiwin
Red Deer
Camrose
Calgary
Bow
Drumheller
Brooks
Lethbridge
Medicine Hat
Crowsnest P.
Kootenay
Trail
Kimberley 1387
Fort McMurray
Athabasca
Lac la Biche
N. Saskatchewan
Lloydminster
N. Battleford
Biggar
Melfort
Prince Albert
Saskatoon
S. Saskatchewan
Swift Current
Moose Jaw
Regina
Weyburn
Estevan
La Ronge
Flin Flon
Sherridon
Churchill L.
Reindeer Lake
Cree L.
Wollaston L.
Lynn Lake
Southern Indian L.
Seal
Churchill
C. Church
Nelson
Thompson
The Pas
Cedar Lake
Norway Ho.
Gods L.
Island L.
Winnipegosis
L. Manitoba
Dauphin
Yorkton
Melville
Portage la Prairie
Brandon
Winnipeg
St. Boniface
Selkirk
L. of the Woods
Kenora
Fort Frances
Rainy
Lac Seul
Sioux Look
Red L.
Red Lake
Sandy L.

UNITED STATES
WASHINGTON
MONTANA
WYOMING
NORTH DAKOTA
SOUTH DAKOTA
NEBRASKA
MINNESOTA
WISCONSIN
IOWA

Milk
Fort Peck
Missouri
Yellowstone
Powder
Little Missouri
Minot
Bismarck
Jamestown
Grand Forks
Moorhead
Fargo
Aberdeen
Pierre
Rapid City
Black Hills 2207
Cheyenne
White
Niobrara
North Platte
Platte
Sioux Falls
Sioux City
Fort Dodge
Mankato
Rochester
La Crosse
Winona
Mason City
Cedar Rapids
Waterloo
Des Moines
Omaha
Grand Island
Minneapolis
St. Paul
St. Cloud
Brainerd
Bemidji
Hibbing
Duluth
Superior
Havre
Bearpaw

Projection: Bonne

ALASKA
1:30 000 000
0   200   400   600 km

RUSSIA
Chukot Ra.
Anadyr
Koryak Ra.
Gulf of Anadyr
Providenya
Bering Strait
Chukchi Sea
Pt. Hope
Kotzebue
Baird Mts.
Brooks Range
Arctic Circle
Prudhoe Bay
Colville
Nome
Seward Pen.
Council
Unalakleet
St. Lawrence I. (U.S.)
C. Romanzof
Norton Sound
Hughes
Circle
Fairbanks
Dawson
Yukon
Kuskokwim
Bethel
Nunivak I.
St. Matthew I.
Pribilof Is.
Mt. McKinley 6194
Alaska Range
Anchorage
Valdez
Wrangell Mts. 4176
Cordova
Kenai
Homer
Seward
Kodiak I.
Kodiak
Alaska Peninsula
Dillingham
Bristol Bay
Kuskokwim Bay
C. Newenham
Karaginski I.
Pt. Barrow
Tanana
Whitehorse
Skagway
Juneau
Sitka
Chichagof I.
Baranof I.
Alexander Archipelago
Ketchikan
Prince of Wales
Prince Rupert
Graham I.
Queen Charlotte Is.
Dixon Entrance
Hecate Str.
Mt. Fairweather 4663
Mt. St. Elias
Yakutat
Montague I.

BERING SEA
GULF OF ALASKA
Aleutian Is.
Unimak I.
Unalaska I.
Umnak I.
Andreanof Is.
Attu Is. 7822
Near Is.
Rat Is.
PACIFIC OCEAN

West from Greenwich

1 : 15 000 000

100   0   100   200   300   400 miles
100   0   100   200   300   400   500   600 km

11   12   13   14   15   A   40   30   B   60

Devon Island
Lancaster Sound
2134
Bylot I.
Pond Inlet   Baffin Bay
Brodeur   Svartenhuk
Peninsula   2136   Peninsula
Gulf   B   a   f   f   i   n
of
oothia   C. Hewett   Disko I.   GREENLAND
Melville   Fury & Hecla Str.   Davis   Strait   Angmagssalik
Peninsula   Prince   Sondre Stromfjord
Charles   I   s   C. Dyer
Foxe   Charles   l   a   n   d
259   Cumberland   Godthaab
Circle   Foxe   Nettilling   Peninsula   C. Mercy   (Nuuk)
Basin   L.   Frederikshaab
Wager   C. Dorchester   Amadjuak   Cumberland Sd.   Juliandhaab   Sydroven
B.   Foxe   L.   Iqaluit   C Farewell   C
Chesterfield Inlet   Penin.   NUNAVUT   3809
Channel   Southampton   Frobisher Bay   A
I.   Coats   Resolution I.   T
Mansel   I.   H   u   d   s   o   n   S   t   r   a   i   t   L
Hudson   I.   Ivujivik   Quaqtaq   C. Chidley   A
King George Is.   Kangiqsujuaq   Akpatok   N   T   50
258   Inukjuak   Amaua   Kangirsuk   I.   1676   Nain   I
Bay   Ungava   Kangiqsualujjuaq   N   E   C
Peninsula   Ottawa   Kuujjuarapik   Ungava Bay   W   C. Harrison
Isv   Feuilles   George   F   Indian Harbour   O
Belcher   Koksoak   Hopedale   Rigolet   Cartwright   C
Is.   Kaniapiskau   O   U   Michikamau   Melville   E
C. Henrietta   Chisasibi   Scheffervile   N   Happy Valley   Battle Hbr.   A
Maria   A   Petitsikapau   D   Goose Bay   N
Lac Bienville   L.   L   a   b   r   a   d   o   r   Str. of Belle Isle   Gander   Bonavista
Severn   Winisk   D   James Bay   Kuujjuarapik   Churchill   Grand   Carbonear
Big   Akimiski   S   Eastmain   L   Labrador City   E   Falls   Newfoundland   St. John's
Trout L.   I.   h   Waskaganish   Q   U   E   B   E   C   1128   Natashquan   Corner   Race
TARIO   Attawapiskat   i   Rupert   1190   Gagnon   B   Mingan   Brook   Grand
Albany   e   Mistassini   Manicouagan   Anticosti   Cabot Str.   aux Basques   C. Race
Moosonee   l   Chibougamau   Sept Iles   I.   Corner   Channel-Port
L. St. Joseph   Missinaibi   d   Baie Comeau   Port-Cartier   Sydney   Glace Bay
Geraldton   Hearst   S   Gouin   R. St. Lawrence   Gaspe   Gulf of   Cape Breton   ST. PIERRE
Nipigon   Hurricanaw   Reservoir   Matane   C. Gaspe   St. Lawrence   New Glasgow   & MIQUELON
L.   Oba   L. Abitibi   La Tuque   Rimouski   Gaspé Pen.   PR. EDWARD I.   Truro   (Fr.)
ipigon   Timmins   Jonquiere   Campbellton   Charlottetown   Dartmouth
Nipigon   Rouyn   Chicoutimi   Riviere   Bathurst   Northumberland Str.   Sable I.
Thunder Bay   Kirkland Lake   Val d'Or   Shawinigan   du Loup   Chatham   Summerside   (Nova Scotia)   6309
ES   Lake Superior   Geraldton   Quebec   Edmunston   NEW   Amherst   NOVA   Bridgewater
Marquette   Sault Ste.   Sudbury   North   Trois Rivieres   St. Hyacinthe   BRUNSWICK   Moncton   SCOTIA   Halifax
Marie   Bay   Cabonga   MONTREAL   Sherbrooke   Fredericton   Saint   Kentville
Sault Ste. Marie   Reservoir   Ottawa   Hull   MAINE   John   C. Sable
WISCONSIN   Georgian   North   OTTAWA   Cornwall   L. Champlain   Bangor   B. of Fundy   Yarmouth
Wausau   Bay   Peterboro   Kingston   Burlington   1917   Lewiston
Green   Lake   Orillia   VERMONT   Portland
NSIN   Bay   Huron   Owen Sound   Oshawa   NEW   Manchester   C. Cod
Appleton   Traverse   TORONTO   Ontario   HAMPSHIRE   Concord
Saginaw   City   Kitchener   Rochester   Syracuse   BOSTON
MILWAUKEE   Niagara   Albany   Springfield   MASS.   Providence
Grand   Hamilton   Falls   NEW   Binghamton   CONN.   RHODE I.
adison   Rapids   London   BUFFALO   YORK   New Haven
ockford   Sarnia   Lake Erie   Scranton   NEW YORK
CHICAGO   DETROIT   Windsor   Erie   PENNSYLVANIA   Newark   NEW JERSEY
ILLINOIS   Gary   INDIANA   OHIO   Toledo   Akron   CLEVELAND   Allentown

West from Greenwich   COPYRIGHT GEORGE PHILIP & SON, LTD

11   12   13   14

HAWAII
1:10 000 000

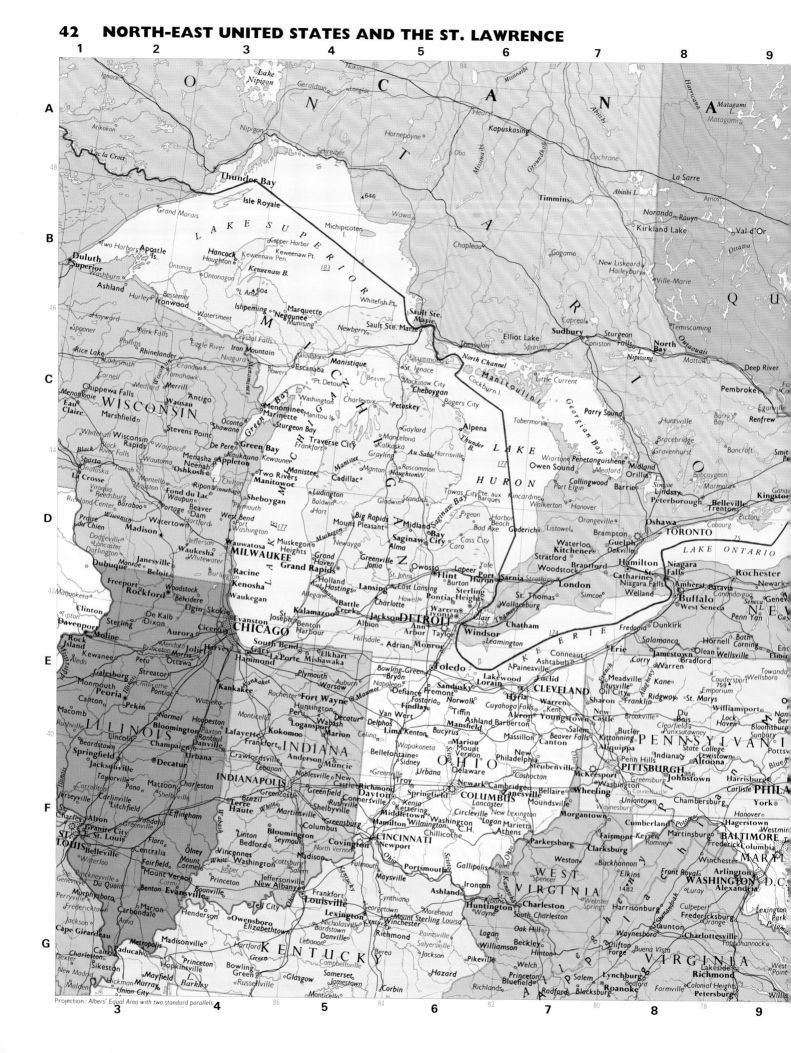

1 : 15 000 000

100   200   300   400 miles
100   0   100   200   300   400   500   600 km

8   9   10   11

A Bermuda (U.K.)
Hamilton

ATLANTIC OCEAN

Columbus
Atlanta   C. Fear
Augusta
Macon
umbus
Charleston
Savannah
bany
hassee   **B**

Jacksonville

Daytona Beach

Orlando   C. Canaveral
Tampa   West Palm Beach
ersburg   Grand
L. Okeechobee   Bahama   **C**
                          I.
Miami   Freeport   Gt. Abaco I.
C. Sable   Fort   New Providence I.
             Lauderdale
Key West   Eleuthera I.
                    Nassau   Cat I.
Florida Str.   S. Salvador
         Andros I.   **BAHAMAS**   Tropic of Cancer
Havana   Matanzas   Long I.
        Cárdenas   Sagua la Grande
Sta Clara   Mayaguana
      Cienfuegos Morón   Acklins
Sancti Spiritus   I.   Turks &
   Ciego de Ávila   Gt. Inagua   Caicos Is.
      B. Camagüey   I.   (U.K.)
         Holguín   Guantánamo
G R E A T E R   Windward Passage
      Manzanillo   Santiago   San Francisco   PUERTO RICO (U.S.A.)
   Bayamo 2000   Cap Haitien   Santiago de Macorís   San Juan   St. Thomas (U.S.A.)
Santiago   Gonaïves   DOMINICAN   Charlotte Amalie
de Cuba   3175   REP.   La Romana   Virgin Is. (U.K.) Anguilla
Grand Cayman   A   N   T   I   L   L   E   S   2280   Baní   St. Martin (Fr. & Neth.)
(U.K.)   Les Cayes   Port au Prince Barahona   Santo Domingo   1338 St. Croix   ST. KITTS & NEVIS
Montego Bay   Hispaniola   Ponce   Caguas   (U.S.A.)   ANTIGUA &
                                                Mayagüez   BARBUDA
JAMAICA   **Kingston**   St. John's
         A   N   T   I   L   L   E   S   Montserrat (U.K.) Guadeloupe (Fr.)
                                                          Leeward   Pointe à Pitre
                                                          Islands   DOMINICA
                                             L E S S E R
                                                    Fort de France   Martinique (Fr.)
Caratasca Lagoon
C. Gracias á Dios   C A R I B B E A N   S E A   A N T I L L E S
                                                 Windward   ST. LUCIA
                                                ST. VINCENT   BARBADOS
                                                         Bridgetown
                                             & THE GRENADINES GRENADA
Providencia   Islands
(Col.)   Pta. Gallinas
San Andrés   Pen. de la   Gulf of Venezuela Aruba (Neth.)   La Blanquilla
(Col.)   Guajira   Curaçao (Ven.)
Bluefields   Santa Marta   Pen de NETH.   Willemstad Bonaire   Margarita   Tobago
agua   Paraguaná ANTILLES   Port of Spain
            Barranquilla   Punto Coro   La Tortuga   Carúpano TRINIDAD & TOBAGO
RICA   Limón   5800   Fijo   (Ven.)   Cumaná G. of San Fernando
        Colón   Sierra Nevada   **Caracas**   Barcelona   Maturín   Paria
Vol. Barú 3374   de Santa Marta **Maracaibo** Maracay
3837   **Panama**   L. de   Cabimas **Valencia**   El Tigre   Ciudad   Georgetown
Azuero   G. of Darién Maracaibo **Barquisimeto**   Orinoco Guayana   New
Coiba   David G. of   Sincelejo   Valera Mérida   Barinas   Ciudad   Amsterdam
        Panama   **Mérida** Cord. de Mérida Apure   San Fernando Bolívar
                 Cartagena   5007   Cúcuta   4100   San Cristóbal de Apure   Cuyuni
                         Barrancabermeja   Arauca Arauca   Angel   Roraima
                 Atrato 3960   **Bucaramanga**   V E N E Z U E L A   Caura Falls 2560
                              Meta   Pto. Ayacucho 2285   Paragua   2810
                 Quibdó **Medellín**   Tunja   Essequibo   1280
                 C O L O M B I A   Sierra Pacaraima
                 Manizales **Bogotá**
                 Pereira   Caquetá
                 Arm-   Ibagué 5215
                 enia   Girardot Guaviare
            Buenaventura   Magdalena
                 Cali 5750   Guaviare   Casiquiare
                 Popayán 4646
                                          B R A Z I L

West from Greenwich   80   9   75   10   70   11   65   12   13

COPYRIGHT. GEORGE PHILIP & SON. LTD.

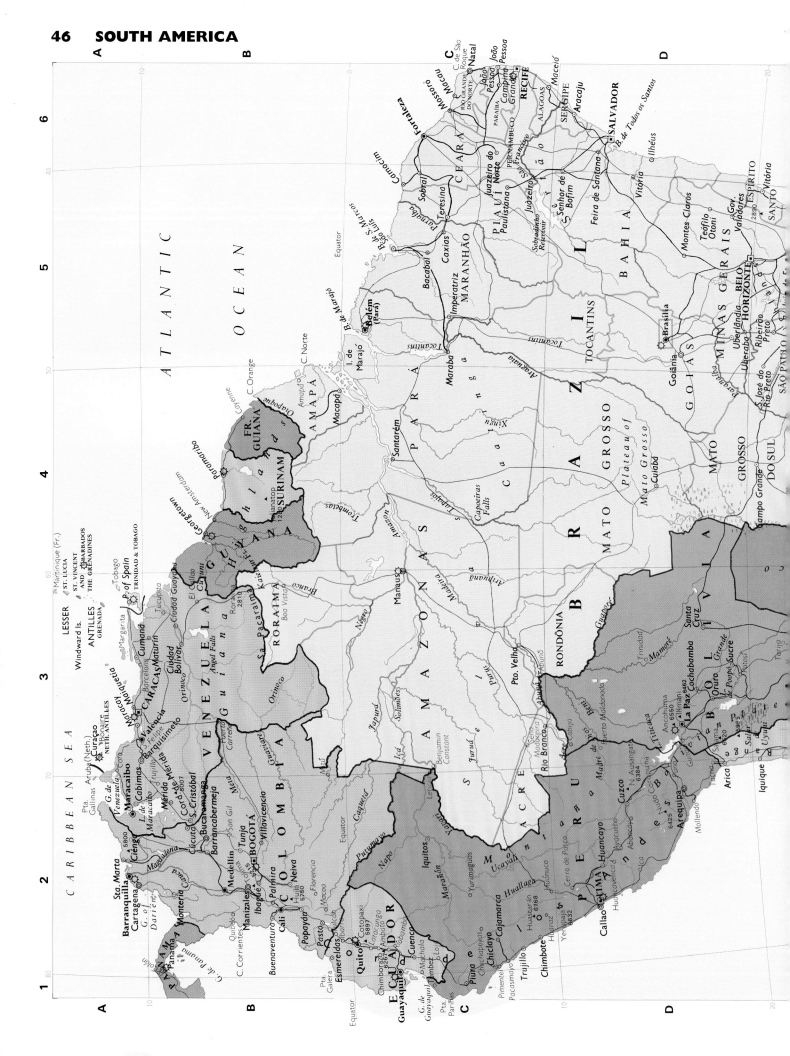

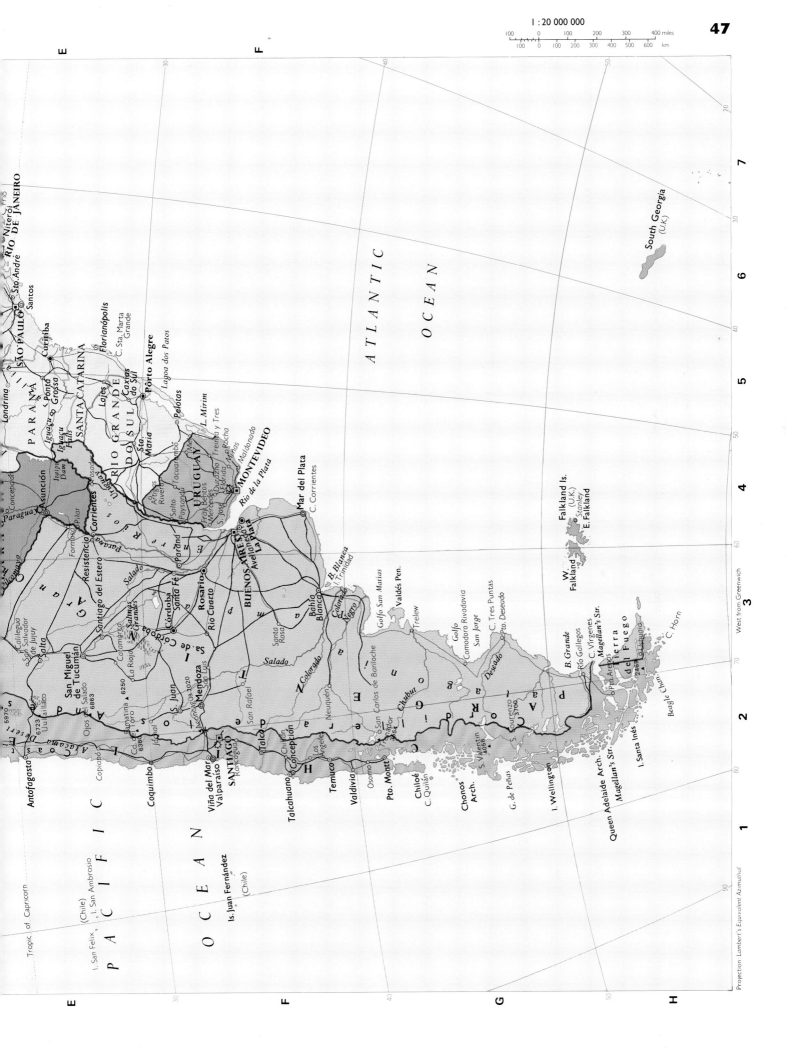

1 : 20 000 000

100   0   100   200   300   400 miles
100   0   100   200   300   400   500   600 km

West from Greenwich

Projection Lambert's Equivalent Azimuthal

ATLANTIC

OCEAN

PACIFIC

OCEAN

Tropic of Capricorn

RIO DE JANEIRO
Niterói
Sto.André
SÃO PAULO
Santos
Curitiba
PARANÁ
Londrina
Ponta Grossa
Iguaçu
Iguaçu Falls
SANTA CATARINA
Florianópolis
Lajes
C. Sta. Marta Grande
RIO GRANDE DO SUL
Caxias do Sul
Pôrto Alegre
Pelótas
Lagoa dos Patos
Sta. Maria
L. Mirim
URUGUAY
Rocha
Treinta y Tres
Melo
Rivera
Tacuarembó
Durazno
Eldrado
Minas
Maldonado
Florida
Mercedes
Paysandú
S. José
MONTEVIDEO
Salto
Artigas
Concepción
PARAGUAY
Paraguay
ASUNCIÓN
Pilar
Formosa
Concepción
Corrientes
Resistencia
Santiago del Estero
Salado
Santa Fé
Sa. de Córdoba
Córdoba
Salinas Grandes
Rosario
Río Cuarto
BUENOS AIRES
Avellaneda
La Plata
Paraná
Río de la Plata
Mar del Plata
C. Corrientes
B. Blanca
I. Trinidad
Bahía Blanca
Colorado
Río Negro
Golfo San Matías
Valdés Pen.
Santa Rosa
Salado
Colorado
San Carlos de Bariloche
Neuquén
San Rafael
Mendoza
Aconcagua 7020
S. Juan
San Luis
La Rioja
Catamarca
Aconcagua 6250
Cd. del Toro 6380
Jachal
Tupungato 6854
Talca
Chillán
Los Angeles
Concepción
Temuco
Valdivia
Osorno
Pto. Montt
Chiloé
C. Quilán
Chonos Arch.
G. de Peñas
I. Wellington
Queen Adelaide Arch.
Magellan's Str.
I. Santa Inés
Talcahuano
Valparaíso
Viña del Mar
SANTIAGO
Rancagua
Coquimbo
Copiapó
Ojos del Salado 6863
Antofagasta
Llullaillaco 6723
Lluta Llailaco 5970
Atacama Desert
I. San Félix (Chile)
I. San Ambrosio
Is. Juan Fernández (Chile)
Calilegua
San Salvador de Jujuy
Salta
San Miguel de Tucumán
Cerro del Salado
P A T A G O N I A
Chubut
Trelew
Golfo
San Jorge
Comodoro Rivadavia
C. Tres Puntas
Pto. Deseado
Deseado
S. Lorenzo 3706
S. Valentín 4058
Río Gallegos
B. Grande
C. Vírgenes
Magellan's Str.
Punta Arenas
Pta. Arenas
Ushuaia
Tierra del Fuego
Beagle Chan.
C. Horn

Falkland Is. (U.K.)
W. Falkland
E. Falkland
Stanley

South Georgia (U.K.)

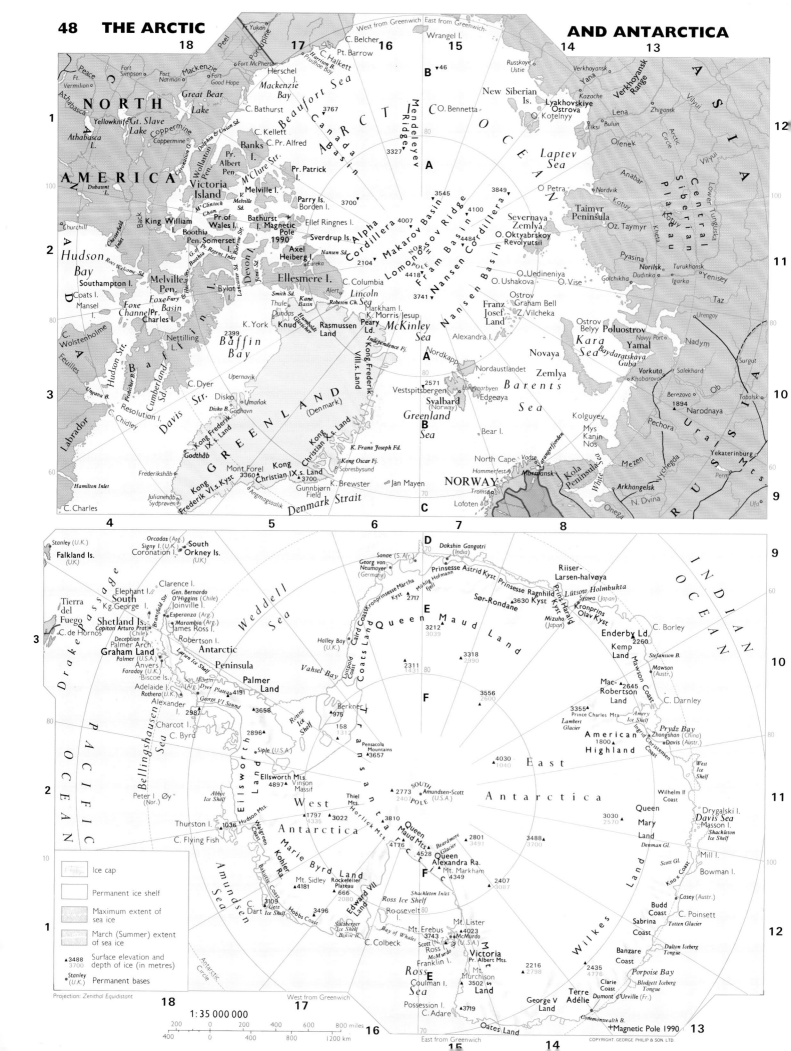

INDEX

The index contains the names of all the principal places and features shown on the maps. The alphabetical order of names composed of two or more words is governed primarily by the first word and then by the second. This is an example of the rule:

New South Wales □ **34** G8
New York □ **43** D9
New York City **43** E11
New Zealand ■ **35** J13
Newark, Del., U.S.A. **43** F10

Physical features composed of a proper name (Erie) and a description (Lake) are positioned alphabetically by the proper name. The description is positioned after the proper name and is usually abbreviated:

Erie, L. **42** D7

Where a description forms part of a settlement or administrative name, however, it is always written in full and put in its true alphabetical position:

Mount Isa **34** E6

Names beginning with M' and Mc are indexed as if they were spelt Mac. Names beginning St. are alphabetized under Saint, but Santa and San are all spelt in full and are alphabetized accordingly. If the same placename occurs two or more times in the index and all are in the same country, each is followed by the name of the administrative subdivision in which it is located. The names are placed in the alphabetical order of the subdivision. For example:

Columbus, Ga., U.S.A. **41** D10
Columbus, Ind., U.S.A. **42** F5
Columbus, Ohio, U.S.A. **42** F6

The number in bold type which follows each name in the index refers to the number of the map page where that feature or place will be found. This is usually the largest scale at which the place or feature appears.

The letter and figure which are in lighter type immediately after the page number give the grid square on the map page, within which the feature is situated. The letter represents the latitude and the figure the longitude. In some cases the feature itself may fall within the specified square, while the name is outside.

Rivers are indexed to their mouths or confluences, and carry the symbol → after their names. A solid square ■ follows the name of a country, while an open square □ refers to a first order administrative area.

Aachen **10** C4
Aalborg **6** G9
Aarau **10** E5
Aare → **10** E5
Aarhus **6** G10
Abadan **24** B3
Abbeville **8** A4
Abéché **29** F9
Abeokuta **30** C2
Aberdeen **7** C5
Abidjan **28** G4
Abitibi L. **42** A8
Abkhazia □ **15** F7
Abohar **23** D5
Abu Dhabi **24** C4
Abuja **30** C3
Acapulco **44** D5
Accomac **43** G10
Accra **30** C1
Acklins I. **45** C10
Aconcagua **47** F3
Acre □ **46** C2
Adamawa Highlands **29** G7
Adana **15** G6
Adapazarı **15** F5
Addis Ababa **29** G12
Adelaide, Australia **34** G6
Adelaide, S. Africa **31** C4
Aden **24** D3
Aden, G. of **24** D3
Adirondack Mts. **43** D10
Admiralty Is. **36** H6
Ado-Ekiti **30** C3
Adoni **25** D6
Adour → **8** E3
Adrar **28** C4
Adrian **42** E5
Adriatic Sea **12** C6
Ægean Sea **13** E11
Afghanistan ■ **24** B5
'Afif **24** C3
Agadès **30** A3
Agadir **28** B3
Agartala **23** H13
Agen **8** D4
Agra **23** F6
Agrigento **12** F5
Aguascalientes **44** C4
Agulhas, C. **31** C3
Ahmadabad **23** H4
Ahmadnagar **25** D6
Ahmadpur **23** E3
Ahvaz **24** B3
Ahvenanmaa Is. **6** F11
Aïr **28** E6
Aisne → **8** B5
Aix-en-Provence **8** E6
Aix-les-Bains **8** D6
Ajaccio **8** F8
Ajanta Ra. **23** J5
Ajaria □ **15** F7
Ajmer **23** F5
Akashi **19** B4
Akita **19** A7
Akola **23** J6
Akranes **6** B2
Akron **42** E7
Aktyubinsk **15** D10
Akure **30** C3
Akureyri **6** B4
Al Ḩudaydah **24** D3
Al Hufūf **24** C3
Al Jawf **24** C2
Al Kut **24** B3
Al Qatif **24** C3
Al 'Ula **24** C2
Alabama □ **41** D9
Aland Is. = Ahvenanmaa Is. **6** F11
Alaska □ **38** B5
Alaska, G. of **38** C5
Alaska Peninsula **38** C4
Alaska Range **38** B4
Alba-Iulia **11** E12
Albacete **9** C5
Albania ■ **13** D9
Albany, Australia **34** H2
Albany, Ga., U.S.A. **41** D10
Albany, N.Y., U.S.A. **43** D11
Albany → **39** C11
Albert L. **32** D6
Alberta □ **38** C8
Albertville **8** D7
Albi **8** E5
Albion **42** D5
Albuquerque **40** C5
Albury **34** H8
Alcalá de Henares **9** B4
Aldabra Is. **27** G8
Aldan → **18** C14
Aleksandrovsk-Sakhalinskiy **18** D16
Alençon **8** B4
Alès **8** D6
Alessándria **12** B3
Ålesund **6** F9
Aleutian Is. **36** B10
Alexander Arch. **38** C6
Alexandria, Egypt **29** B10
Alexandria, La., U.S.A. **41** D8
Alexandria, Va., U.S.A. **42** F9
Algarve **9** D1
Algeciras **9** D3
Algeria ■ **28** C5
Algiers **28** A5
Alicante **9** C5
Alice Springs **34** E5
Aligarh **23** F7
Alipur Duar **23** F12
Aliquippa **42** E7
Aliwal North **31** C4
Alkmaar **10** B3
Allahabad **23** G8
Allegan **42** D5
Allegheny → **42** E8
Allegheny Plateau **42** G7
Allentown **43** E10
Alleppey **25** E6
Allier → **8** C5
Alma **42** D5
Almaty **18** E9
Almelo **10** B4
Almería **9** D4
Alor **22** D4
Alpena **42** C6
Alps **10** E5
Alsace **8** B7
Altai **20** B4
Altay **20** B3
Altoona **42** E8
Altun Shan **20** C3
Alwar **23** F6
Amadjuak L. **39** B12
Amagasaki **19** B4
Amarillo **40** C6
Amazon → **46** C4
Ambala **23** D6
Ambikapur **23** H9
Ambon **22** D4
American Samoa ■ **35** C17
Amiens **8** B5
Amman **24** B2
Amos **42** A8
Amravati **23** J6
Amreli **23** J3
Amritsar **23** D5
Amroha **23** E7
Amsterdam, Neths. **10** B3
Amsterdam, U.S.A. **43** D10
Amudarya → **18** E7
Amundsen Gulf **38** A7
Amundsen Sea **48** E1
Amur → **18** D16
An Najaf **24** B3
An Nasiriyah **24** B3
An Nhon **22** B2
Anadyr **18** C19
Anadyr, G. of **18** C20
Anaheim **40** D3
Anambas Is. **22** C2
Anantnag **23** C5
Anar **24** B4
Anatolia **15** G5
Anchorage **38** B5
Ancona **12** C5
Anda **21** B7
Andalucía □ **9** D3
Andaman Is. **25** D8
Anderson **42** E5
Andes **46** E3
Andhra Pradesh □ **25** D6
Andorra ■ **9** A6
Andreanof Is. **38** C2
Ándria **12** D7
Andros I. **45** C9
Angara → **18** D11
Ånge **6** F11
Angel Falls **46** B3
Angerman → **6** F11
Angers **8** C3
Anglesey **7** E4
Angola ■ **33** G3
Angoulême **8** D4
Angoumois **8** D3
Anguilla ■ **44** J18
Anhui □ **21** C6
Anjou **8** C3
Ankara **15** G5
Ann, C. **43** D12
Ann Arbor **42** D6
Annaba **28** A6
Annapolis **42** F9
Annecy **8** D7
Annobón **27** G4
Anshun **20** D5
Antalya **15** G5
Antananarivo **33** H9
Antarctic Pen. **48** D4
Antibes **8** E7
Anticosti I. **43** A16
Antigua & Barbuda ■ **44** K20
Antofagasta **47** E2
Antsiranana **33** G9
Antwerp **10** C3
Anyang **21** C6
Aomori **19** F12
Aoraki Mt. Cook **35** J13
Apeldoorn **10** B3
Apennines **12** B4
Apia **35** C16
Appalachian Mts. **42** G7
Appleton **42** C3
Aqmola = Astana **18** D9
Ar Ramadi **24** B3
Arabian Desert **29** C11
Arabian Gulf = Gulf, The **24** C4
Arabian Sea **24** D5
Aracaju **46** D6
Arad **11** E11
Arafura Sea **22** D5
Aragón □ **9** B5
Araguaia → **46** C5
Arak **24** B3
Arakan Yoma **25** C8
Aral **18** E8
Aral Sea **18** E8
Arcachon **8** D3
Arctic Ocean **48** B17
Arctic Red River **38** B6
Ardabil **24** B3
Ardennes **10** D3
Arendal **6** G9
Arequipa **46** D2
Argentan **8** B3
Argentina ■ **47** F3
Arima **44** S20
Arizona □ **40** D4
Arkansas □ **41** D8
Arkansas → **41** D8
Arkhangelsk **14** B7
Arles **8** E6
Arlington **42** F9
Arlon **10** D3
Armenia ■ **15** F7
Arnhem **10** C3
Arnhem Land **34** C5
Arnprior **42** C9
Arrah **23** G10
Arran **7** D4
Arras **8** A5
Artois **8** A5
Aru Is. **22** D5
Arunachal Pradesh □ **25** C8
Arusha **32** E7
Asab **31** B2
Asahigawa **19** F12
Asansol **23** H11
Asbestos **43** C12
Asbury Park **43** E10
Ascension I. **27** G2
Ashkhabad **18** F7
Ashland, Ky., U.S.A. **42** F6
Ashland, Ohio, U.S.A. **42** E6
Ashtabula **42** E7
Asifabad **23** K7
Asir □ **24** D3
Asmara **29** E12
Assam □ **23** F13
Assen **10** B4
Assisi **12** C5
Astana **18** D9
Asti **12** B3
Astrakhan **15** E8
Asturias □ **9** A3
Asunción **47** E4
Aswân **29** D11
Atacama Desert **47** E3
Atbara **29** E11
Atbara → **29** E11
Athabasca → **38** C8
Athabasca, L. **38** C9
Athens, Greece **13** F10
Athens, U.S.A. **42** F6
Atikokan **42** A2
Atlanta **41** D10
Atlantic City **43** F10
Atlantic Ocean **2** E9
Atyraū **18** E7
Au Sable → **42** C6
Aube → **8** B5
Auburn, Ind., U.S.A. **42** E5
Auburn, N.Y., U.S.A. **42** D9
Aubusson **8** D5
Auch **8** E4
Auckland **35** H13
Aude → **8** E5
Augrabies Falls **31** B3
Augsburg **10** D6
Augusta, Ga., U.S.A. **41** D10
Augusta, Maine, U.S.A. **43** C13
Aunis **8** C3
Aurangabad, Bihar, India **23** G10
Aurangabad, Maharashtra, India **23** K5
Aurillac **8** D5
Aurora **42** E3
Austin **40** D7
Australia ■ **34** E5
Australian Alps **34** H8
Australian Capital Territory □ **34** H8
Austria ■ **10** E8
Autun **8** C6
Auvergne **8** D5
Auxerre **8** C5
Avallon **8** C5
Avellino **12** D6
Avignon **8** E6
Ávila **9** B3
Avranches **8** B3
Axiós → **13** D10
Ayers Rock **34** F5
Ayr **7** D4
Azamgarh **23** F9
Azerbaijan ■ **15** F8
Azores **2** C8
Azov, Sea of **15** E6
Azuero Pen. **45** F8

Babol **24** B4
Babuyan Chan. **22** B4
Bacău **11** E14
Bacolod **22** B4
Bad Axe **42** D6
Badajoz **9** C2
Badalona **9** B7
Baden-Württemberg □ **10** D5
Baffin I. **39** B12
Baghdad **24** B3
Baguio **22** B4
Bahamas ■ **45** C10
Baharampur **23** G12
Bahawalpur **23** E3
Bahía = Salvador **46** D6
Bahía □ **46** D5
Bahía Blanca **47** F3
Bahraich **23** F8
Bahrain ■ **24** C4
Baia Mare **11** E12
Baie-St-Paul **43** B12
Baikal, L. **18** D12
Baja California **44** B2
Bakersfield **40** C3
Bakhtaran **24** B3
Baku **15** F8
Balabac Str. **22** C3
Balaghat **23** J8
Balaton **11** E9
Balboa **44** H14
Baldwin **42** D5
Balearic Is. **9** C7
Baleshwar **23** J11
Bali **22** D3
Balikeşir **13** E12
Balikpapan **22** D3
Balkan Mts. **13** C10
Balkhash, L. **18** E9
Ballarat **34** H7
Balqash **18** E9
Balrampur **23** F9
Balsas → **44** D4
Baltic Sea **6** G11
Baltimore **42** F9
Bam **24** C4
Bamako **28** F3
Bamberg **10** D6
Bamenda **30** C4
Bancroft **42** C9
Banda **23** G8
Banda Aceh **22** C1
Banda Is. **22** D4
Banda Sea **22** D4
Bandar Abbas **24** C4
Bandar Khomeyni **24** B3
Bandar Seri Begawan **22** C3
Bandundu **32** E3
Bandung **22** D2
Bangalore **25** D6
Banggai Arch. **22** D4
Bangka **22** D2
Bangka Str. **22** D2
Bangkok **22** B2
Bangladesh ■ **23** H13
Bangor **43** C13
Bangui **32** D3
Bangweulu, L. **32** G6
Banja Luka **12** B7
Banjarmasin **22** D3
Banjul **28** F1
Banks I. **38** A7
Bankura **23** H11
Bannu **23** C3
Banská Bystrica **11** D10
Banyak Is. **22** C1
Baoding **21** C6
Baoji **20** C5
Baotou **21** B6
Bar Harbor **43** C13
Bar-le-Duc **8** B6
Baracaldo **9** A4
Baramula **23** B5
Baran **23** G6
Baranovichi **11** B14
Barbados ■ **44** P22
Barberton, S. Africa **31** B5
Barberton, U.S.A. **42** E7
Barcelona **9** B7
Barddhaman **23** H11
Bardstown **42** G5
Bareilly **23** E7
Barents Sea **48** B8
Barhi **23** G10
Bari **12** D7
Bari Doab **23** D4
Barisal **23** H13
Barito → **22** D3
Barkly Tableland **34** D6
Barkly West **31** B3
Barletta **12** D7
Barmer **23** G3
Barnaul **18** D10
Barques, Pt. aux **42** C6
Barquísimeto **46** A3
Barrancabermeja **46** B2
Barranquilla **46** A2
Barre **43** C11
Barrie **42** C8
Barry's Bay **42** C9
Bashkortostan □ **14** D10
Basilan **22** C4
Baskatong, Rés. **43** B10
Basle **10** E4
Basque Provinces = País Vasco □ **9** A4
Basra **24** B3
Bass Str. **34** H8
Basse-Terre **44** M20
Bassein **25** D8
Basseterre **44** K19
Basti **23** F9
Bastia **8** E8
Bata **32** D1
Batangas **22** B4
Batavia **42** D8
Bath, U.K. **7** F5
Bath, Maine, U.S.A. **43** D13
Bath, N.Y., U.S.A. **42** D9
Bathurst, Australia **34** G8
Bathurst, Canada **43** B15
Batna **28** A6
Baton Rouge **41** D8
Battambang **22** B2
Batticaloa **25** E7
Battle Creek **42** D5
Batu Is. **22** D1
Batu Pahat **22** C2
Batumi **15** F7
Bavaria = Bayern □ **10** D6
Bawean **22** D3
Bay City **42** D6
Bayamo **45** C9
Bayan Har Shan **20** C4
Bayern □ **10** D6
Bayeux **8** B3
Bayonne **8** E3
Bayrūt **24** B2
Beacon **43** E11
Beagle, Canal **47** H3
Béarn **8** E3
Beauce, Plaine de la **8** B4
Beaufort Sea **48** B18
Beaufort West **31** C3
Beauharnois **43** C11
Beaumont **41** D8
Beaune **8** C6
Beauvais **8** B5
Beaver Falls **42** E7
Beaver I. **42** C5
Beawar **23** F5
Béchar **28** B4
Beckley **42** G7
Bedford, Ind., U.S.A. **42** F4
Bedford, Va., U.S.A. **42** G8
Bei'an **21** B7
Beijing **21** C6
Beira **33** H6
Békéscsaba **11** E11
Bela **23** F1
Belarus ■ **11** B14
Belau = Palau ■ **36** G5
Belaya Tserkov **11** D16
Belcher Is. **39** C12
Belém **46** C5
Belfast, S. Africa **31** B5
Belfast, U.K. **7** D4
Belfast, U.S.A. **43** C13
Belfort **8** C7
Belgaum **25** D6
Belgium ■ **10** C3
Belgorod **15** D6
Belgrade **13** B9
Beliton Is. **22** D2
Belize ■ **44** D7
Belize City **44** D7
Bellaire **42** E7
Bellary **25** D6
Belle-Ile **8** C2
Belle Isle, Str. of **39** C14
Bellefontaine **42** E6
Belleville **42** C9
Bellingshausen Sea **48** D3
Bellinzona **10** E5
Belmopan **44** D7
Belo Horizonte **46** D5

 AFGHANISTAN

ALBANIA

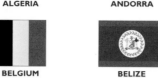 ALGERIA

 ANDORRA

 ANGOLA

ANTIGUA & BARBUDA

 ARGENTINA

BARBADOS

BELARUS

BELGIUM

BELIZE

BENIN

 BHUTAN

BOLIVIA

BURUNDI

CAMBODIA

 CAMEROON

CANADA

 CAPE VERDE

 CENTRAL AFRICAN REP.

CHAD

CROATIA

CUBA

CYPRUS

CZECH REPUBLIC

DENMARK

 DJIBOUTI

 DOMINICA

 ETHIOPIA

FAROE ISLANDS

FIJI

FINLAND

FRANCE

 GABON

 GAMBIA

GUINEA

GUINEA-BISSAU

GUYANA

HAITI

 HONDURAS

 HONG KONG

 HUNGARY

ITALY

IVORY COAST

JAMAICA

JAPAN

 JORDAN

 KAZAKSTAN

 KENYA

LEBANON

LESOTHO

 LIBERIA

LIBYA

 LIECHTENSTEIN

 LITHUANIA

LUXEMBOURG

MALTA

 MAURITANIA

 MAURITIUS

 MEXICO

 MICRONESIA

 MOLDOVA

 MONACO

NEW ZEALAND

NICARAGUA

NIGER

NIGERIA

 NORTHERN MARIANAS

 NORWAY

 OMAN

 PORTUGAL

 PUERTO RICO

QATAR

ROMANIA

RUSSIA

 RWANDA

SAN MARINO

SLOVENIA

SOLOMON ISLANDS

SOMALIA

SOUTH AFRICA

SPAIN

 SRI LANKA

ST KITTS & NEVIS

SYRIA

 TAIWAN

 TAJIKISTAN

TANZANIA

THAILAND

TOGO

 TONGA

 UNITED ARAB EMIRATES

UNITED KINGDOM

 UNITED STATES

URUGUAY

UZBEKISTAN

VANUATU

VATICAN CITY